WHO
STOLE
MY
MOJO?

WHO STOLE MY MOJO?

HOW TO GET IT BACK AND LIVE, WORK AND PLAY BETTER

GARY BERTWISTLE

CAPSTONE

Other Wiley Editorial Offices

John Wiley & Sons Inc., 111 River Street, Hoboken, NJ 07030, USA

Jossey-Bass, 989 Market Street, San Francisco, CA 94103-1741, USA

Wiley-VCH Verlag GmbH, Boschstr. 12, D-69469 Weinheim, Germany

John Wiley & Sons Australia Ltd, 42 McDougall Street, Milton,
Queensland 4064, Australia

John Wiley & Sons (Asia) Pte Ltd, 2 Clementi Loop #02-01, Jin Xing
Distripark, Singapore 129809

John Wiley & Sons Canada Ltd, 6045 Freemont Blvd. Mississauga,
Ontario, L5R 4J3 Canada

Wiley also publishes its books in a variety of electronic formats. Some
content that appears in print may not be available in electronic books.

British Library Cataloguing in Publication Data
A catalogue record for this book is available from the British Library

ISBN 978-1-90646545-2 (PB)

Typeset in 10.5/14 pt by SNP Best-set Typesetter Ltd., Hong Kong
Printed and bound in Great Britain by TJ International Ltd

CONTENTS

To my baby girl Charley, for showing me a world
full of possibilities, through the eyes
of a child . . . forever yours.

iNTRODUCTiON

It was during the closing presentation of the International Alliance of Learning Conference in Washington DC, USA, in 2006 that the concept for this book first came to me. I was thinking over the fantastic presentations that I had attended at the conference and the new and valuable information and training techniques that I had gained, and it occurred to me that while many of the attendees sitting in the room would leave the conference feeling motivated and inspired, within weeks all but a few would find themselves back in their old routines wondering what had happened to that extra spark they had felt during their time away. Where did their motivation go? Why did all their new ideas come to nothing? In fact, the question in their minds will be, 'What happened to my Mojo?' I am sure that many of you have experienced something similar.

Throughout our lives, we are often exposed to new concepts, ideas, methodologies and outlooks. However, after the initial excitement and stimulation wears off we often find our motivation dies away and all that enthusiasm comes to nothing. Then we look back and ask ourselves, 'What happened to my Mojo?'

When I arrived home and spoke to friends and family about the book concept I was surprised to discover just how interested everyone was in learning more about their Mojo. No matter how successful or happy a person seemed, it soon became apparent that everyone wanted to learn more about how to increase their Mojo.

WHAT iS MOJO?

Why Mojo? What in fact *is* Mojo? Mojo can be defined as your magic, voodoo, charm, or your energy, vitality, zest, drive, zip, zing, spirit, verve, pizzazz, punch, passion, oomph, power, get up and go, vigour and feistiness.

There is no doubt that people from all walks of life are losing their zip and their spark. It seems that the little bit of extra energy that we need to get the most out of life is sadly lacking in a lot of people. I believe this lack of Mojo is really important to address as it affects every aspect of our lives . . . our mood, our relationships, our emotions, our work, our play, our creativity, and in turn it affects our results and what we get out of life.

Mojo is the extra spark that is the difference between having a good day and a great day. It's the difference between getting good results and outstanding results. You know yourself when you are in the presence of someone with Mojo. They just seem to have that extra something that helps them get that little bit more out of any situation.They seem centred and calm, yet at the same time they have that twinkle in their eye - they have Mojo.

SO WHY DO YOU NEED MOJO?

Why is Mojo so important? Because it gives you the edge. It gives you the spark, oomph and energy to wring the last bit of juice out of your life. Without Mojo life has a tendency to be bland and mediocre. But once you get your Mojo working and put that vitality and vigour back into your life, the rewards come tenfold. People with Mojo seem to attract different and better results, and they always seem to find themselves in the right place at the right time in order to gain that extra inch. The greatest achievers in any aspect of life - be it business, family, sport, politics, religion or community - are the people who achieve the most and live their life to the fullest . . . people with Mojo.

Mojo comes in many different disguises and this book will give you the essential keys to unlock yours. Mojo is within all of us - the trick is knowing how to access it. Once you access your Mojo, you can not only put that something extra into your life, you also gain a great deal more. Every day, ordinary people are doing extraordinary things, and you can be one of them if you choose to be.

Our attitude and the way we think determines everything we do, and in this book I hope to be able to give you all the essential information and tools you need in order to get the most out of your life. But remember that unless you change the way you think, everything will stay the same - mental and physical vibrancy must be earned and this book will show you how to acquire yours.

WHO'S GOT MOJO?

Sometimes Mojo may seem out of reach of the everyday person, however I'm sure all of us know somebody that we live with, work with or hang out with who has it. Think about the people around you who have that spark, energy, and extra bit of oomph, and then think about what attributes they have. That's what this book is about. It's finding those special ingredients that separate those who have Mojo from those who don't.

Who Stole My Mojo? is full of simple tips and tools, examples and anecdotes that I've collected from some of the thousands of people I've met and worked with over the years who all have Mojo. It's also full of observations about people who quite obviously have lost their Mojo. My question is, what gives people their Mojo? And for those who might have lost it, how do they get it back?

I've purposefully written this book in short, simple chapters so that you can take a single concept and apply it to your own world in an instant. The book is packed with practical ideas about how to foster Mojo in your life and, most importantly, to make sure that no-one steals it from you ever again.

If you carry this book around with you while you are reading it, my suggestion would be that when you have a spare moment to drop your shoulders and relax, you can pull it out and read a chapter. I'd then encourage you to ponder what you've read, throw it around, wrestle with it, sleep on it, but most importantly apply it. Before you know it, you'll be at the end of the book and the people around you will be looking at you and saying - you've got Mojo!

THE BACK SECTION

Although this is not a workbook as such, I believe that there are some valuable nuggets you will find as you move through the book.

One thing I find with this type of book is that if you seem to find a number of tools, tips or bits you want to implement, it's impossible to do them all at once. The real value of this book is that it is a resource tool that you can go back to time and time again, and by having one reference page at the back of the book, it enables you to periodically go back and implement the pieces in stages.

For example, as you go through a chapter you might find a number of pieces that you want to implement, but rather than feel as though you have to do them all at once, when you are reading, or complete the book, you can stage them out over a number of weeks or months, in order to ensure that you implement them at some time. The biggest mistake people make is trying to do too much too quickly, when merging these new action steps into their current busy lifestyles. You'd be much better off to stagger your ideas over a period of time in order to merge them successfully into your current life.

As you go through the book, there are certain areas that you may want to make notes on and I have made a reference to the appropriate area in the back of this book for capturing those nuggets.

At the back of the book you'll find plain note pages for you to capture your own thoughts, queries or notes as well as specific action boxes that relate to parts of the book. You'll also see that I've made a space for a six stage plan. You could make each stage either a week or a month - the timing is entirely up to you. But as you go through the book, spread out your action so that you can try something, get it working, then go back to stage 2, try that and get it working as well.

This book is written as a resource so that at any given time you can go back to it and identify where you lost your Mojo. At the end of each chapter you'll also find a type of checklist, which is a series of questions to ask yourself in order to determine where you lost, or even who stole, your Mojo. It's not so much a chapter summary, but more a checklist that you can go back to on a monthly, quarterly, half yearly, or yearly basis.

I hope you find these additions to the book of benefit; it's a method that has helped me in my reading, evaluation and implementation of books, and my hope is that it continues to increase the value of the book that you have in front of you.

CHAPTER 1

MOJO MiNDSET

I am sure that every one of you knows someone who you would say has Mojo. If I asked you to list what qualities these people possess that you believe gives them their Mojo, quite often the list includes such things as leadership skills, initiative, spark, adventure, fun, liveliness, contagiousness and spontaneity. Now I don't believe, nor do most of the attendees at conferences that I have run, that there is anything on that list that you can't do yourself or you couldn't have more of in your life if you really wanted to. That is because having Mojo is largely a state of mind. People with Mojo always seem to see things differently than those who are struggling to find theirs.

For example, what do you see when you look at the illustration below?

I3

The context in which you see this figure will largely depend on what you see. Some people will see the number 13 . . . but others may see the letter B.

A, **B**, C, D

12, **B**, 14, 15

What do you see in the following picture?

To some it's just a stick. But to others it's an extra-ordinary solution to many of life's problems.

Once again different people see different things. And this is also true with the Mojo mindset.

I was working with a group at a conference in Melbourne recently and I flew with the attendees from Sydney to Melbourne on a 7 a.m. flight. Given the early check-in, everyone was required to be up and out of bed between 4.30 and 5 a.m., and by early afternoon people were starting to think about their long day and complain about the early start. Then somebody challenged the group by saying that this was a great opportunity to encourage a Mojo mindset.

People with Mojo tend to be excited at the prospect of getting up at that hour because they believe they are getting a two-hour jump on those who are dragging themselves out of bed at 7 a.m. They choose to see it as a positive that they have an extra two hours in their day, week and in fact their life. Yet, the people without Mojo complained because they missed out on their sleep. Did the people who got up at 5 a.m. feel any different to those who got up at 7 a.m.? Maybe, maybe not. But you'd have to agree that their more positive mindset would make all the difference in how they approached their day and to the people they interacted with during that day.

Now I'm not saying that it's a matter of running around proclaiming that the world is perfect and that everything is great. It's about understanding that whenever something happens or an opportunity presents itself, you and you alone have the choice of how you will react to it. Life is a lot like playing a game of cards. Sometimes you're dealt a good hand and sometimes you're not. But either way your reaction to the hand you are dealt has a direct bearing on your Mojo. It also explains why great poker players, even though they have a poor hand, are able to bluff their opponents to take the pot. Instead of seeing a bad hand they instead see an opportunity to bluff. I guess this is where the term 'poker face' comes from. We as a society have been taught from a young age to identify the negatives or the things that are wrong. Consequently when we are dealt our hand in life we tend to focus on the negatives as opposed to the positives. Developing a Mojo mindset is all about appreciating your hand, and understanding that regardless of whether you have a good hand or a less-than-brilliant hand, it is how you approach it and what you do with it that makes all the difference.

Not long ago I had an uncle who was in the final stages of a long battle with cancer. I went with my mother to visit him in hospital during his last days, essentially to say goodbye. This was without a doubt one of the hardest and most emotional things I've ever had to do.

Before I went to see him I thought about what I was feeling and the emotions that were going on inside me. I thought to myself there were two ways I could approach the situation. Either I could go in terribly upset because I was there to say goodbye, or I could go in and celebrate the last few hours I would spend with this courageous man and endeavour to put a smile on his face and the faces of the close family in the room. I chose to enjoy this valuable time with him, and not concern myself with what was yet to happen.

It turned out to be a good choice, as my uncle improved slightly and went on to live a further three weeks, and I was able to visit him on more than one occasion to spend precious time together and to laugh and share stories. That mindset choice enabled me to enjoy the quality time we spent together, and those moments will live with me forever.

In the coming sections I will share with you some simple and practical tools to enable you to develop a Mojo mindset approach in your own life.

PURE THINKING

'Three minutes of pure thinking is what we're after.' That's what Rod the spin class teacher asked for during a cycling class I was attending at the gym one Thursday night. The moment he said those words it struck me that I had been thinking about everything except what I was in fact doing. As soon as he said 'pure thinking', I started to concentrate on my cycling technique, trying as hard as I could to cycle effectively. After the class as I sat outside cooling down, I thought more about the term pure thinking, and realised that it's a talent that people with Mojo definitely possess.

In this day and age, especially with younger generations increasingly growing up surrounded by new technologies, the opportunities for moments of quiet contemplation on any one subject are becoming more and more difficult to find. Each morning when I take my young daughter Charley for a walk around the block in her pram, I see a teenage girl who sits waiting for a lift to school. Every morning (and I mean *every* morning) I see that girl chatting away on her mobile phone to friends. It would be nice to see her spend some time just pondering or watching the world go by rather than filling every spare minute talking with others. I believe that we should be encouraging pure thinking in all its forms (such as the gentle art of contemplation or day dreaming) to stimulate our imagination, which we can use for things such as problem solving. People with Mojo often seem to have plenty of time on their hands and are always clear when it comes to a new or innovative way of solving a problem or issue. Pure thinking is about emptying your mind of everything else and concentrating on one thing and one thing only. It may only take three minutes, but you'd be surprised at how much more you'll create and how much better your imagination will be when you are focused on just one thing.

A great example of the difference pure thinking can make comes from a scene in the film *The Last Samurai*, in which Tom Cruise's character is attempting unsuccessfully to learn to fight with a samurai sword. A young Japanese boy walks up to Tom's character and gives him some advice - he says, 'Too many mind.' Tom Cruise looks at him with a puzzled expression. The young boy then says, 'Mind on sword, mind on opponent, mind on people watching, too many mind. No mind.' At that point Tom Cruise's character makes an effort to empty his mind of everything except working with the sword, and he experiences much greater success. It is one of my favourite scenes in the movie, and one I think of when I find myself trying to do too many things at once rather than just doing one thing and doing it properly.

Another great example of the value of pure thinking comes from an interview I recently watched with the great golfer Jack Nicklaus, who is still on the competitive golf circuit at well over 60 years of age. During the interview Jack's fellow players all commented on Jack's ability to shut out competitors, the audience, noise, and any other distractions, and just concentrate on what was at hand, whether that was hitting, putting, or driving the golf ball, to great success. Here is a man who is in his 60s, and certainly has his Mojo working.

By adopting a pure thinking approach you can make better use of your Mojo and get it working for you. Whether at the gym, at the office, in a conversation with your best friend or mum, or enjoying a book, try to empty your mind of the clutter of your thoughts and your daily life and use pure thinking to concentrate on one thing and one thing only - purely.

POSITIVES, POTENTIALS AND CONCERNS

No matter what life throws at them, people with Mojo are able to step back from problems and view them from a different, more positive perspective. You can do the same using what I call 'Positives, Potentials and Concerns', or PPC. Before heading straight for the negatives or things that are wrong with a situation, try

PPC. Research has shown that from the time we are young children we hear almost three times more negative comments and commands than positive affirmations, and predominantly these come from those closest to us - parents, teachers, coaches and friends. Consequently, by the time we reach adulthood, when something happens and we're faced with an issue or problem we automatically revert to a mindset of asking what is wrong or what might go wrong in that particular situation. PPC turns this on its head and gives your thinking some much needed Mojo.

The next time you are faced with an issue, rather than exploring all the things that are wrong, or looking at the negative side, first consider the positives. What's good about the situation, and what is going right (Positives)? Once you've considered the positives, you then need to look at the potential for the concept (Potentials). If some changes were made, what might you be able to do with it? If the situation is in fact negative, would it be possible to change things and make it into a positive? And then finally you can approach the concerns and the things that are troubling you (Concerns).

If you focus on the concerns first, you're basically closing yourself off to potential opportunities you may have been presented with and you may be shutting down potentially good ideas with all the reasons why it won't work before you even get started. Don't be a party pooper who enjoys bringing down other people's ideas by focusing on what's wrong with them - leave that to others.

By looking at the positives first you can bring Mojo back into your office, business, circle of friends, family, and social circumstances. This PPC process is more than just positive thinking. It's a way of giving your imagination, ideas and thinking a chance to breathe new life, as well as injecting it into those around you. Whenever you're faced with a challenging concept or a problem, first consider the potential that lies within it and what could be done to turn it around.

PPC is a wonderful tool. Many organisations I've worked with have changed their entire corporate culture by employing this method of thinking. On a personal front, many individuals I know have also brought much happiness and Mojo into their personal lives by considering firstly the positives and potentials in their relationships before they move on to deal with other issues that may be affecting them in a negative way.

YOUR GiFT

Discovering your gift will have a lasting impact on the level of Mojo in your life. It was during a break at a seminar at which I was presenting that I was fortunate enough to meet a delightful lady who brought home the importance of this. We had been discussing the day's speakers and the conference in general, but towards the end of our conversation she told me the story of her son who had been severely injured in a car accident while riding his bicycle. Her son had been a very successful young football player, however as a result of the accident he had become a paraplegic and was now wheelchair-bound. The amazing thing about her story was that she was smiling as she told it! She then went on to say that her son as a result of his new circumstances had discovered he had a talent for web design, and was now a very well recognised graphic designer in his field.

The point his mother wanted to make was that although he would naturally have liked to have found his gift while he was able bodied, he believes that had he not had the accident he would never have found his gift and an outlet for the incredible creativity and imagination he was able to offer others. For him the accident was the catalyst for discovering something about himself that he never knew existed.

In a perfect world we would all discover our gift without having to go through such a traumatic experience, but it seems to me that a large proportion of the population don't discover their gift or make significant changes in their life until something dramatic happens, if at all. You have the opportunity *today* to discover your gift - why wait for a health scare, an accident, a job loss or other such event to start the ball rolling? The conversation I had that day was a gift in itself to me. You have to admire her son, you have to admire his mother, and you have to admire the human spirit, in the way he managed to take good from an event that would physically and mentally have destroyed a lot of people.

Don't wait to discover your gift; take the time and spend the energy to find yours now!

CHOICES

One of the things you will notice about people who have strong Mojo is that they always believe they have choices in life, and this is very empowering. As the PPC process demonstrates you always have a choice as to how you view things in life. People who have their Mojo working know that whatever happens they have a choice as to how they interpret or react to something. These people love life and are out to experience as much as they possibly can in the time they have available. As Muhammad Ali is reported to have said, 'We have less time than you think.'

In the interview I referred to earlier with Jack Nicklaus he was asked why he was always so strong in the last round of a tournament, when most of his competitors seemed to be falling in a hole. Actually for golfers, the problem is probably the ball *not* falling in the hole. Jack's response was that the night before any final round of a tournament he always visualised his competitors coming unstuck and that he would be the only one in the tournament who wouldn't. By choosing to believe that he was not going to be the one to make mistakes, it gave him great power, confidence and the energy he needed going into the last round.

Jack knew he couldn't control the other players. He could only control himself - his own thoughts, his mind, and the attitude he took into his game, which was that he would be the strongest player on the course.

He said he saw it, he believed it, he embedded it into his psyche, and today he is known as one of the great golfers of our time. We can all learn something from his experiences, but most important of all is to remember that we all have the power to choose how we react in any given set of circumstances in life.

Love her or hate her, there is no question that Joan Rivers, the TV presenter and celebrity interviewer, is a larger-than-life character. She has survived decades in Hollywood, the ups and downs of TV, the harsh words of critics and the burden of celebrity for more years than I think I've been alive. In a recent interview with Michael Parkinson, Joan Rivers made the following comment: 'I've been fired, I've been thrown out. I've been told I'm over. I've been told five times "Forget about her" . . . but you keep coming back. So an audience doesn't like me. It makes you sad, but I know there's a tomorrow and that makes a big difference.' What an attitude. Here is a woman who has put up with more negativity than most of us could endure in a lifetime, yet at this year's Emmy Awards she conducted her 1000th celebrity interview on the red carpet! Without question Joan knows that she is not loved by everyone and that not everything she has done over the years has been a great success, but she chooses to look at life in a positive manner and look at where it has taken her.

Michael Jordan is regarded by many as being the greatest basketball player in the history of the game, and in some people's view one of the greatest sportsmen the world has ever seen. When, in one of his many interviews over the years, Jordan was asked why he was as good as he was, he replied that he had modelled himself on another United States basketball player named Julius Erving, often known as Dr J. He said Dr J held himself to a standard higher than any other person or player could ever hold themselves to. And so that became Jordan's mantra - to hold himself to a standard higher than anyone else could ever possibly ask of him. He was always the first person onto the court at training, and the last person to leave. He took more shots at training than any other player, because he knew that some time soon he would be called upon to deliver that winning shot on the buzzer, and when the time came he wanted to know he could do it. And this meant he had to work, train and play harder than anybody else. This attitude was a choice. He wanted and aspired to be more than just a good player - he wanted to be the best. This was his particular Mojo mindset. He made a conscious decision to set himself apart, to ask more of himself, to be and do more than others - and look at his rewards. You couldn't say that Michael Jordan doesn't have Mojo.

There's an old saying about lemons and I believe it is very appropriate to this chapter. People without Mojo see lemons as lemons. People with Mojo take lemons and make them into lemonade. People with Mojo want more. They won't settle for mediocrity - it simply does not work for them. Above all it is about choice. You can either be like most of the world or you can set yourself apart and ask, be and do more.

THE CONTROLLABLES

After giving a keynote address at a conference I had the pleasure of dining with another of the speakers, a former Olympian and Commonwealth Games gold medal winner. We spoke at length about her athletic career, and over the course of our conversation she explained how injury had plagued her so often during her career.

On one occasion she said she was lying on the massage table during a treatment discussing her latest injury with her coach. The injury was frustrating her incredibly, and it was starting to lead her to question her ability. Her coach could see how the injury was affecting her and began to ask her a series of questions. He asked whether she'd been having her regular massage, if she'd been doing her stretching, whether she'd been icing the injury, whether she'd been attending her physiotherapy and chiropractic appointments, and whether she'd been doing the exercises given to her by the physiotherapist. She was able to respond with an emphatic 'Yes' to all his questions. He then asked if there was anything else she could possibly be doing to help the injury mend more quickly, to which she replied no, she was doing everything she possibly could.

At this point, the coach said, 'Then forget about it and relax.' Quite surprised, she asked, 'What do you mean? The championships are only weeks away and I'm still injured!' Calmly he replied, 'Control the controllables. If you're doing everything you can to put yourself on the road to recovery, and there's nothing more you can do, then just relax and control what you can control. The things that are now out of your hands are in the hands of mother nature, and will take their own course.'

I believe that this is wonderful advice and a great premise to carry with us in our daily lives. Too often we find ourselves getting caught up with issues and frustrations over which we have absolutely no control. Sitting in traffic, waiting for a bus that is running late, or impatiently waiting for a client to attend a meeting can be terribly frustrating occurrences for all of us. However, if there is nothing you can possibly do to change the situation, then there is absolutely no value in stressing, worrying or losing energy over it. This will only deplete your Mojo. Remember you can only control the controllables. Do whatever is possible to improve the situation, but once you've done all you can, simply relax and focus your energy onto something more productive.

In his book *The Seven Habits of Highly Effective People*, Stephen Covey describes what he calls Circle of Influence and the Circle of Concern. His recommendation is to spend more time on the things you can influence that will take you towards your goals, and less time on the things that concern you but in effect you cannot control and ultimately will not help you achieve your goals.

I am constantly amazed by the number of people who tell me they don't have enough time in their day. Yet when you ask them to do a stock-take of how they've actually occupied their hours, you tend to find they have invested a lot of time and energy into activities that are really of no value to them and do not bring them any closer to achieving the goals they may have set for themselves in their day, week or life. Never confuse activity with accomplishment. Too many people busy themselves in a circle of concern and spend little or no time on the things that they can influence or control. People who have Mojo focus on accomplishment and their circle of influence, and seek only to control the controllables.

RiSiNG SUN

People with Mojo don't walk around pointing the finger of blame at others. Rather than blaming others, they get on and fix the problem. In the movie *Rising Sun* starring Wesley Snipes and Sean Connery, there is a particular scene that sums up this sentiment beautifully. Sean Connery is talking to Wesley Snipes, and says, 'Blame, who's to blame? Fix the problem not the blame.' Find out what's gone wrong and fix it. No one is to blame. We are always trying to find out who messed up. Their way is better.

This concept of fixing the problem not finding blame is well known in Japanese culture and is one we should adopt more often. The attitude of blame is unfortunately very prevalent in many corporate organisations, and even in some social circles. Quite often I hear audiences talk about the politics and finger-pointing that goes on in companies, and I find it really disappointing as all it does is suck the creativity, inspiration, motivation and Mojo from not only individuals and teams but also the organisation in general.

In the book *The 10 Rules of Sam Walton - Success Secrets for Remarkable Results*, the author Michael Bergdahl recounts many memorable stories about Sam Walton, known affectionately by his team as Mr Sam. In one of the sections 'Communicate With People and Show You Care', he said that Mr Sam believed in spending his time solving problems, not wasting it trying to affix blame. This is probably why even with two million staff worldwide Mr Sam was idolised by each and every one of them. He was a people person who got on with doing the job, as opposed to affixing blame and pointing the finger. If you think back to Stephen Covey's theory on the circle of influence and circle of concern, those who point fingers and appoint blame are clearly working in a circle of concern, whereas those who get on and fix the problem, therefore moving themselves towards their goals, are working in the circle of influence. Once again it comes down to choice and whether you choose to have a Mojo mindset or not.

SEE YOUR MOJO

There is no question that the power of the mind and the power of visualisation are quite extraordinary.

When you have a dream, a challenge, a job to do, or you're attempting anything at all in your life, you firstly need to close your eyes and picture it. Picture it vividly, picture a positive outcome, and you'll be amazed at the influence this has on the result.

I was fortunate enough on one occasion to meet Marilyn King, three-time US Olympic representative in the pentathlon. During the course of our conversation we talked about how Marilyn went about her preparations for the Olympic Games. Marilyn recalled the build-up to her third Olympic Games, where only a matter of months before the USA selection trials she was in a very bad car crash. For three months she was restricted to her bed and was unable to train.

However, during that time, Marilyn found every Olympics or athletics video tape she could for her event, and watched them over and over again. She said she eventually became so tired of watching them that she even started to play them backwards just for a kick! The whole time she was restricted to her bed, she never stopped visualising what it would be like to be able to compete in her third Olympic Games.

Once she was mobile again, Marilyn began going to the track, but as she was still unable to train, she would stand at the start line at the track and ask people to set up the hurdles for her. Marilyn said that with her eyes closed she was able to visualise herself jumping the hurdles. She would then hobble down to the high jump, have someone set up the high jump bar, and then visualise herself scaling the high jump. At the Olympic trials that year, not only was Marilyn able to compete, she was actually placed second, and made the Olympic team for her third time - and she had done this without a single day of training. The only training she had done was in her mind!

Now you don't need to be an Olympian for the power of visualisation to work for you. I had a client, Rob, who really wanted to improve his golf game. About six months earlier Rob's wife had had a baby and consequently he was not playing a lot of golf. I worked a lot with Rob visualising how he wanted his swing to look, what the game would feel like, and the score that would be on the board when he left the course. Over a period of months Rob's golf handicap dropped from almost a seven to less than four (and it wasn't a bad handicap to start with). But what's most outstanding is that Rob had achieved it by playing less golf! The only practice he had been doing was in his mind. Although not an Olympian, Rob achieved his goal and experienced an overwhelming sense of satisfaction at the improvement he was able to bring to his golf game - which certainly says something for the power of visualisation even in our everyday lives!

Walt Disney always said, 'If you can dream it, you can do it.' I once read a story about Roy Disney, brother of the incredibly creative Walt, who on the day that Walt Disney World opened to the public in Florida was driving a journalist around the park in a golf buggy. Unfortunately Walt had died before Walt Disney World was completed, and at the end of his tour of the new theme park, the journalist turned to Roy and said, 'This is fantastic, isn't it a shame that Walt never saw it?' Roy just smiled at the journalist and said, 'Walt did see it, that's why you're seeing it today.'

If at any time you want to think about what the future will look like, or you want to think about a great idea, simply close your eyes and dream. Draw vivid pictures in your mind of whatever your dream for the future may be. The fascinating thing about the human mind is that it can't determine what is fact or what is fiction. So when you create a clear picture in your mind of a dream, a goal, or a problem you're about to solve, the brain treats it the same whether it's happened or not. When you visualise yourself with the energy and Mojo you desire, the brain will then go about searching for evidence and information to back up your thought or vision. There's an old saying, 'Act the way you want to become, until you become the way you act.' But you can't become it until you can see it. Visualisation is a very powerful thinking tool that can be used to help you get more spark, energy and results out of your world. Visualise yourself with Mojo and it will be so.

There is a documentary called *When We Were Kings*, about the incredible Rumble in the Jungle boxing match between Muhammad Ali and George Foreman in Zaire. The focus of the media and even Ali's entourage would always be on the huge dints left by George Foreman's thumping punches in the heaviest of punching bags. Ali trained after Foreman each day in Zaire, but he chose not to focus on the punching bag, but instead think about all of the children and hardship in the less privileged areas of his country and the world he believed he was fighting for. He could see the enormous impact that he would have by beating George Foreman and setting an example for children and people all over the world of what was possible. Where most would have focused on the sheer power and ferociousness of George Foreman, Muhammad Ali instead focused on the good that would filter through the world when he won the fight.

You can visualise good things, or you can visualise and focus on the negatives. Most people are very good at visualising and focusing on what they *don't* want to happen or the hardships that lie ahead. Take a tip from Muhammad Ali, and focus only on the things that you want to happen, and the reasons why. 'I am the greatest. I said that even before I knew that I was.' And so he is.

Many successful business and sports people, and even actors, visualise an event or situation occurring before it actually happens in order for them to get into the right state of mind. It's a tool that each of us can use, and you need no props. You just need to be able to relax and imagine what the future will look like. You need to imagine yourself with Mojo.

As George Lucas, the creator of the *Star Wars* series, said during an interview on *60 Minutes*, 'If you can't imagine it you can't do it. And if you can't imagine yourself doing it, you can't do it.' The first step towards building Mojo is the ability to imagine and to see yourself with Mojo.

What would you be like with Mojo in your world?

PROBLEMS, PROBLEMS, PROBLEMS

While working in Japan with a large television production company I was able to spend some time with the

CEO of the organisation. During our conversations we discussed various aspects of creative thinking, and the processes involved in problem solving and generating new ideas for television. This CEO said that his favourite pastime was sitting back in his chair with his feet up on the desk, just thinking. I liked him from the very start! He then said that as much as people often looked strangely at him when he said this, he loved any opportunity he had to really sit back and think.

Now this doesn't sound all that different to many of us who enjoy the opportunity to flex our creative muscles, but here's why I thought his creative process was so different, and why it undoubtedly contributed to his Mojo.

He surprised me by saying how much he loved to be approached with problems! He loved it when a client, supplier or staff member came to him with a problem. Naturally my question to him was, 'Why is that?' He said that when someone approaches him with a problem it gives him a chance to think . . . really think. He said that too often he was so caught up in the everyday activities of the business that he never really had a chance to challenge how things might be done differently or to find an innovative new way to solve a problem. And this is why he relished the opportunity so much when it arose.

This is a very surprising attitude to take, and certainly one that if you can manage to get right, creates great Mojo. No doubt it is one of the reasons he is the CEO of one of the largest television organisations in Japan. No matter what you do in life, both in and out of the workplace, problems are inevitable. But as we discussed earlier in the book, what is important is *how* you choose to approach these problems. I think it's a worthwhile exercise for all of us to take a step back and think about how we approach problems. Ask yourself - do you see your problems as being a huge inconvenience or do you see them as an opportunity to flex your creative muscles and find a solution? To really get your Mojo working, look at your problems differently and reframe them. How you approach and think about a problem is probably the most important part of the problem-solving process.

One of my favourite quotes comes from self-help guru Dr Wayne Dyer, who said, 'As you think, so shall you be.' If you look at the positive side of a problem or issue then that is how you will approach it. Conversely, if you believe that bad things are going to happen, then bad things probably will. If you approach problems as a challenge and a real chore, that's exactly what they become, and inevitably this will suck your Mojo before you've even started to think about a solution. So next time you are faced with a problem, try thinking about it as an opportunity to exercise your creative muscles and increase your Mojo in the process.

GET OUT MORE

Getting out more does amazing things for your Mojo. Take a moment to think about where you were when you came up with some of your great ideas. Audiences I have worked with all over the world have remarkably similar responses, such as the car, the gym, walking the dog, relaxing with friends, drinking in the pub, cooking, at the movies, sitting in the bathtub, or even on the toilet! I'm sure that if you compare your answers to these you would find that there are similarities, and chances are that the locations you have on your list are the places where generally you are most relaxed. Unfortunately for a lot of people, they spend the majority of their time in the workplace in front of their computer or jammed in a boardroom, which really doesn't make sense if you want to get your creative mind and your Mojo working. Creative ideas come to you when you drop your shoulders and are completely relaxed . . . which is why a lot of ideas come to us in our sleep. If you want to get your Mojo working and increase your creativity, imagination and problem-solving then you need to get out more and spend more time in the places where you are most relaxed.

Does this scenario sound familiar - answering your phone while checking your emails, flicking through your diary and pulling out that file before the next meeting . . . all while trying to shovel a sandwich into your mouth? With all the tension, distractions, multitasking and stress in our daily lives it's little wonder that your Mojo is being stolen away.

One suggestion that I have for you to get your Mojo ideas going is to do what the Romans used to do, 'Solvitas perambulum - Solve it while you walk'. When looking for a new idea or trying to solve a problem, get out of your seat, push yourself away from the board-room table, release yourself from the computer and walk.

Simply by standing up you will increase the oxygen to your brain by ten per cent and this can certainly help get your Mojo mindset right when creating new and interesting ideas and solving problems. Your mind works better creatively when it's relaxed and open to the things around you. Whether you're surrounded by crowds of people, sitting quietly under a tree, having a coffee in a coffee shop or even walking through the streets, you need to make the time to allow your ideas to flow. I have spoken with stay-at-home mothers who have arranged for their baby or child to be looked after so that they can clear their head and get out of the house for an hour to two.

Fresh air, walking, exercise, or even sitting some-where in the shade and just pondering does amazing things for your Mojo, and ultimately will also increase your ability to generate great ideas. When you're expe-riencing a mental block or you need clarity on an issue, get out. Go and sit in a park, do some people-watching or grab a cup of coffee and take some big deep breaths. You'd be surprised at how quickly your Mojo starts to work. Find that place or those places where your ideas and imagination are most stimulated and make sure you visit them on a daily basis.

Poet Robert Frost once said, 'An idea is a feat of association.' When you take yourself away from the office or the familiar surroundings of home you can usually open yourself up to a lot more interesting and exciting ideas through the stimulation and association of new surroundings. Whether you call them associations, stimulants or triggers, what you're really looking for are items, events, people, colours, shapes or designs that will activate your creative mind and ultimately your Mojo.

When your creativity and imagination are stimulated and you find a new or interesting way of doing something, it's an amazing feeling. So what are you waiting for? Get up and get out!

CHANGE YOUR iDENTiTY

I had the pleasure of attending a four-hour swim class with former world record holder and Olympic and Commonwealth Games gold medallist John Konrads. At one time Konrads held thirty-two world records, as well as the world record for every distance in the pool from 100 metres to 1500 metres, so he knows a bit about swimming.

During the class I thoroughly enjoyed the opportunity to sit back, listen and learn from an expert. The fact that I was learning new information on a topic I knew very little about was terrific. I could feel my brain being stretched, and my desire to learn being motivated. However, it was something else that John said that I thought was really relevant to this whole idea of a Mojo mindset.

During the swim session John spoke of a swim coach who at the time was working with one of Australia's finest swimmers, Ian Thorpe. The philosophy of this coach was to train based on times that were slightly faster than the actual ones. For example, assume Thorpe was swimming 2 minutes 40 seconds (2:40) for a particular event; they would train as if Ian Thorpe is a 2:30 swimmer who is currently swimming 2:40. I thought this was brilliant! It means that his swimmer has the belief that he's actually a 2:30 swimmer. He is programming the swimmer's brain to be a 2:30 swimmer and basing everything he does in his training sessions around the fact that he already is.

It's the same principle that people who want to lose weight or achieve a goal might use. If you put a drawing, photo or written copy of the expected goal or outcome on a mirror, automatically the brain will set about programming you towards that success, and because you can see it, you really start to believe it. What you're actually doing is changing your identity from what you are to what you want to be, and because the brain does not know the difference between what's real and what's imaginary, it sets about finding evidence to back up and ensure that what you're seeing as your new identity actually becomes reality.

I have adopted this philosophy in both my running and my work, and I can say with confidence that it certainly makes a difference when you are open to the concept as you are able to program your brain to operate, see and think in a different way. For example, in a business sense, if you were to say, 'I'm a General Manager but I'm currently doing the job of the senior account person', then automatically you start to think, behave, learn and act more like the General Manager because in your own mind you believe that's the level at which you are operating.

Don't allow your *perception* of your identity to create a ceiling over your current or potential ability.

If you think back to Rob, the golfer I spoke about earlier, my challenge was to get him to see himself as a three or four handicap player, not a seven or eight handicap player. My first barrier was getting him to change his thinking, and then secondly to prove to himself that he could in fact do it. His identity had always been based around playing second fiddle to the club's best players, and although he dreamed of it, he never really believed in his own mind that he could play at a three or four level. That belief was all he needed to start the process of change.

Recently I had arrived early to a conference at Melbourne Zoo at which I was presenting. I was near the zoo entry looking for some guidance, and I asked a cleaner who happened to walk by whether she knew where I might go. She simply shrugged her shoulders, looked embarrassed, and said, 'I'm sorry I'm unable to help you, I'm just a cleaner.' This is a classic example of someone who has created an identity for themselves in their own mind and has certainly created ceilings over their ability and their potential. She was not *just* a cleaner, and could have seen herself as an ambassador for the zoo, as well as a huge contributor to the safety and future of animals both in and out of the zoo if she chose to. How you see yourself is a choice that is entirely in your own hands.

In contrast, I remember having a conversation with Frank, the cleaner who is responsible for maintaining the floors in my creative venue called the Ideas Vault at the Entertainment Quarter in Sydney. The venue has its own coffee shop and supermarket, and with a high traffic flow through the venue, we need to have our floors cleaned quite regularly. Twenty years ago Frank and his wife Maria came to Australia as immigrants, unable to speak a word of English. They settled in Sydney and began working as cleaners. As time passed they were able to afford to buy a small house, from which they have since upgraded three times, and they now live in a beautiful house with their children in one of Sydney's outer suburbs. The house Frank and his family live in now is really something, and Frank is very proud of it - and the fact that he owns it outright!

As well as this, Frank now also owns property on the north coast of Australia in one of our premier tourist areas! I would suggest that the majority of people would walk past Frank and see just a cleaner, but Frank has not taken on the identity of *just* a cleaner, and as a result he has set himself up very comfortably for the future. His dream is to one day, when his children are old enough, sell the property and spend the rest of his life travelling around the world with his wife Maria. What a great story, and certainly one that is contrary to what most people would expect to hear about a cleaner. Frank made a choice about how he viewed his identity - and he set himself no limits!

Changing your identity need only be done in your own mind. It's a way of conducting yourself, it's a way of thinking, it's the levels you hold yourself to, and ultimately it's about self-confidence and self-esteem. It is not something you need to openly brag about. You just need to know how you see yourself every day when you go to work, play sport, or interact with friends, and your brain will search for evidence to help you back that up.

Another great example of having a strong identity from a very early age is Canadian singer Michael Bublé. In an interview on the Biography Channel, he said that from an early age he had absolutely no doubt that he would be famous. He could see it, hear it, and feel it. Every time he picked up a microphone, he saw himself being on stage in front of crowds of people, crooning like his heroes. Every time he walked on stage, even from an early age, he was a star. There's an old saying that if you want to change the fruit, you must first change the roots. If you want to change the visible, you must first change the invisible. Change your identity and become the person you want to be, and see your Mojo build.

A good example of changing an identity comes to us from an outstanding Australian swimmer, Leisel Jones. During the 2004 Olympics in Athens Leisel finished with the silver medal in her pet event - the 200 metre breast stroke. Now a silver medal for anyone in the Olympic Games is an outstanding achievement, but Leisel had set her sights very high, so that when she only won silver, in her own mind she was desperately disappointed. The Australian media were very harsh in their criticism of Leisel and how she handled winning the silver medal. Whether it was right or wrong, they accused her of behaving like a spoilt brat when accepting the medal in front of the world.

Within a matter of a year however, Leisel came out and won a gold medal for the same distance, winning her race by half a pool length and smashing the world record at the same time. Australian commentators said that it was one of the greatest swimming efforts they had ever seen, and when she left the pool to the roaring approval of the audience, Leisel was all smiles. When Leisel was interviewed immediately after the race on the pool deck, what I found interesting was her reflection on the disappointment of her Olympic Games performance. She said, 'I can see now that I hated the person I was back then, but I changed everything, and I love the person I am now.'

I believe Leisel is a wonderful role model in the way she now conducts herself both in and out of the pool. Not only is she a champion athlete, but her identity, personality, desire and determination are without question. She is a wonderful young Australian who is a great ambassador for both her sport and her country.

Another interesting example of identity is pop diva Beyonce Knowles, a solo artist and a member of the hugely successful Destiny's Child. Beyonce revealed that she becomes someone else when she goes on stage, in her mind she calls her stage persona 'Sasha'. When asked why, she said, 'Because when I'm on stage, that's not who I really am. I'm not confident, I'm not strong enough to do that job, its just not me.' But when

Beyonce goes on stage believing that she is Sasha, she has no problems in wowing the world with her music, songs, moves and dance routines.

This is something you can try in your own mind in one of your many pursuits. When you are making a presentation, or in front of a church audience, or giving a speech at the Christmas table, create a new persona and give that persona an interesting name.

I quite often use a similar technique when running creative sessions with groups. When they're generating ideas for their group I have them imagine they're Walt Disney and ask them what Walt would do in a particular situation. Then we'll run through people like Gandhi, Oprah Winfrey, Shane Warne or Richard Branson and have the audience pretend they are one of those people. In changing their identity they're changing their thinking.

One of my favourite television programs in recent times has been the crime show *CSI*. The character of Gil Grissom, the boss of the Crime Scene Investigation unit in Las Vegas, is brilliantly written. He is portrayed as a highly intelligent, highly skilled and dedicated investigator, but at the same time, he comes across as very human. In one particular episode Grissom made the following comment that had me running to my journal to write it down. He said, 'What we are never changes. Who we are never stops changing.' *What* you are - your DNA - won't change, but *who* you are *can* change as of this minute. Your identity as it is now can be changed. Don't try to be something you're not, but simply work out who you want to be and go about becoming it. Act the way you want to become until you become the way you act.

Remember that from your choices come actions and from your actions come results. You have a choice. If you are reading this book you obviously feel that someone has stolen your Mojo. In order for you to steal it back, something has to change. After reading this book hopefully you'll make some choices, and from those choices will come action. But unless you take action you'll get no results. As Einstein once said, 'Nothing happens until something moves.'

Now it's your move.

TAKE THAT BACK

Many years ago I had worked with one of the founders of the Westfield shopping centre group, John Saunders, whom I greatly admired. Unfortunately John passed away a few years ago, but a book by Gabriel Kune was written about his life called *Nothing is Impossible*, which I found fascinating.

What I found of particular interest was the story of what Saunders did as a newly arrived young Hungarian Jew in Australia. Apparently when he found a Hungarian–English dictionary and came across the entry for *impossible*, he scribbled it out with a red pen so that it was totally illegible. From that moment forward, whenever he spoke to bank managers, financiers, partners, or people in the street and they told him that what he wanted was impossible, he would simply pass them the dictionary and say, 'If you can show me the word impossible in there, I'll back off.'

In Saunders' mind, nothing was impossible, and he had removed that word totally from his vocabulary. Having worked with John for many years and witnessed the achievements of this incredible man, not only in shopping centres and other industries, but also in his contribution back to the community, I could see where this stemmed from.

In 2005 I remember watching the ESPN Sports Awards on cable television. Each year the ESPN representatives from around the world award a prize in recognition of courage, which is called the ESPY award. In 2005 it was given to a less able-bodied athlete called Jim MacLaren. During the introduction for the award Oprah Winfrey stated that Jim MacLaren had also removed the word *impossible* from his vocabulary.

Jim is an unbelievable athlete who has faced more hardship and tragedy than you and I could ever imagine, yet he has defied doctors with his achievements. After not one but two serious accidents involving himself, motor vehicles and bicycles, Jim found himself hospitalised and told by doctors that he would never move from the neck down again. Yet defying modern medicine (many doctors are calling him a living miracle), he is now able to walk with assistance, and cycle in a gymnasium. It defies logic what Jim has achieved and is achieving, but it has come about because he has removed the word *impossible* from his vocabulary.

Having seen and heard many inspiring stories such as these, I started thinking about my own world and the words that I wanted to erase from my own vocabulary. As a result, words such as 'can't' and 'sick' no longer exist in my personal vocabulary. As I've said before, the brain doesn't know the difference between what is real and what is imaginary, so when you program yourself through language and speech both internally and externally, your brain will search for evidence to back up those statements.

If you consistently tell yourself you can't do something, every time you find yourself in difficulty, your brain will say, 'See I told you, you can't do this.' If, on the other hand, nothing is impossible and there's nothing you can't do, then your brain will search for ways to help you achieve that end. If you take the words out of your vocabulary, the brain has nowhere to go.

To bring Mojo into your life, get rid of the words that steal your Mojo away. Grab a piece of paper or write in the back of this book three words that you will personally remove from *your* vocabulary. They could be words such as 'scared', 'fear', 'can't', 'should' . . . whatever will be most empowering to you.

If the words no longer exist in your vocabulary, your brain will have no way of latching on to the negativity. It is a very empowering exercise, and by removing those words that perhaps have created a ceiling in your life you are free to be whatever you want to be. If you tell yourself you can, or you tell yourself you can't, either way you are right.

FORGET ABOUT iT

It's believed that almost eight out of ten employees lose sleep thinking about work, or find themselves obsessing about work during their personal time. I can tell you right now that this is one thing that is guaranteed to sap your Mojo. People with Mojo have that uncanny ability to find synergy between work and play.

A simple tool that can help you steal back your Mojo is what I call 'Forget about it'. Now I don't mean that you should ignore issues that need to be addressed, but my suggestion is that you temporarily forget about whatever it is that you need to think about and let your subconscious ponder it for a while before you come back to it at a later time, when your subconscious has had time to work on the issue.

Have you ever noticed that when you are thinking about buying a new car and you decide on a particular model, when you're driving around the following week, that model is all you seem to see? Or when you set your alarm to get up in the morning for a special occasion, that you automatically wake up one minute before the alarm. Why is that? Because the subconscious mind is thinking about what it is you are choosing to buy, or is setting up an internal alarm clock to wake you up at a specific time. There's a whole science behind this that I won't go into, but just know that your subconscious mind can be an incredible tool if you make the best use of it. So how do you do that?

Your subconscious mind is like a giant cook pot. The best way to use it is to put all the information into it, put the lid on, walk away, let it simmer, and come back to it at a later time - it's just like cooking a stew. If you're at work and you have a problem or situation that is worrying you or needs to be addressed, simply jot down some notes regarding the issue, and when you're done, put the pen down, turn the page over and literally forget about it. Go back to it in a couple of hours or days (depending on how much time you have) and check in. You will be surprised at what solutions and answers you'll have found while you've been consciously working on something else. Once you place an idea in your subconscious mind it quietly goes about finding solutions and ideas while consciously you can get on with other things.

The subconscious is always a source of fascination to me, and this exercise is definitely worth trying as it is something that works for a large number of people. The more you use it the better you will become at using it. Remember the important thing is to record the information then forget about it and come back to it in an hour, two hours, or a day later and see what you've got.

If you are worried about something or would like to come up with some ideas before you go to sleep, jot down your thoughts, clear your mind, have a think about it, then say to yourself I'm going to forget about this now and get some sleep. Once you lie down, if the thought comes back to you, just say to yourself, 'Forget about it, I'll worry about it tomorrow.' At that point your subconscious mind goes to work.

You may find yourself waking up during the night; if so, write down the solutions or ideas that come to mind on your piece of paper. Trust me, you won't remember them the next day if you don't write them down. The same thing applies as soon as you wake up in the morning - roll over and write down whatever is going on in your mind, because two minutes later it is too late and the idea is gone forever. When you wake up, your subconscious mind will have done the thinking for you, while you feel nice and rested. It's a great way to start the day.

You may not think that using the subconscious mind is something that will work for you, but take this scenario as an example of how your subconscious mind goes to work without you even being aware of it. Say you were at a dinner party and someone asked you the name of a particular actress in a film you saw some time ago, and for the life of you, you can't think of her name, although you know you know who it was. An hour later, while dessert is being served, suddenly the name comes to the top of your mind and you shout it out loud. In astonishment, everyone looks at you and asks what on earth you're talking about. You then tell them the background to the story and that the answer has just come to you.

How did that happen? Well we don't really know for sure, but that is the power of the subconscious mind. This use of the subconscious can work in any situation, at any time of the day. People with Mojo don't dwell eternally on issues - they think about it, put it to rest, and come back to it at a later stage. By using your subconscious to deal with problems or to come up with solutions, you will free up your mind, put yourself back in control of your life, and in the process steal back your Mojo.

LET GO

Below is an excerpt from a book by T. Harv Eker, called *Secrets of the Millionaire Mind*:

> A man is walking along a cliff and all of a sudden he loses his balance, slips and falls off. Fortunately he has the presence of mind to grab onto the ledge, and is hanging there for dear life. He hangs and hangs and finally he yells out, 'Is there anybody up there who can help me?' But there is no answer. He keeps calling and calling, 'Is there anybody up there who can help me?' Finally this big bellowing voice calls back, 'This is God, I can help you, just let go and trust.' Next thing you hear is, 'Is there anybody else up there who can help me?'

The lesson we can take from this story is simple. If you want to move to a higher level of life, you have to be willing to let go of some of your old ways of thinking and adopt new ones. The results will eventually speak for themselves. In order to steal back your Mojo you may have to let go of some old thinking. Many people have been conditioned over the years to believe certain things about their identity, their potential, and where they believe they are going in the future. In order to steal back your Mojo often you need to let go of your old thinking and start to create a new identity and a new Mojo mindset. In his book, T. Harv Eker discusses how often people will have a blueprint or identity in their mind of their potential for wealth creation. Most people put a ceiling over their earning capacity, and most people I meet would never believe they could be millionaires or truly financially well off.

Most people only think about their next pay cheque, or what their annual salaries are, as opposed to building true wealth and designing the life they want to lead. They are caught up in what society says they should be; that is, struggling, working, putting money in the bank and living pay cheque to pay cheque. Being a millionaire, a multimillionaire, or a billionaire is simply a matter of designing a blueprint for yourself, or as we discussed earlier in this chapter, creating an identity for yourself that you are happy with.

The example Eker's book gives is contrasting your blueprint for financial success against that of Donald Trump's. If Donald Trump had a net worth of 'only' one million dollars, how do you think he'd feel about his financial success? Most people would agree that he'd see himself as being a financial failure. Yet for most of us if we had a net worth of a million dollars it would be an enormous amount of money and we'd feel like we had achieved a great deal. As you can see, it all depends on your individual identity, your own blueprint, and whether or not you have your own Mojo mindset in place.

During a presentation that I call 'Raise the roof', I often make reference to the ceilings people place over themselves. Ceilings can happen in all areas of life, and people are particularly good at placing ceilings or limits over their own wealth creation. If you think it is only possible for you to earn X dollars per annum, then that's exactly what you're going to program yourself for. However, if you look ahead and say you're worth X plus Y, then you are creating for yourself a new identity. I'd encourage you to think about your own plan, your own capabilities, the ceilings that up till now you have been placing over yourself, and what you would like your identity for the future to be. Take the time to ask yourself what your new Mojo blueprint is going to be. One million dollars is just a ceiling as we all know, and by removing the ceiling, you open yourself up to incredible possibilities in all areas of your life.

If you see yourself as always being single but you yearn for a partner, then remove that ceiling and build your new identity and your Mojo mindset around creating the perfect world, the ideal partner, and doing the things that make you happiest in life. There is no reason why you cannot be a multimillionaire, have the perfect partner, the ideal family, own an incredible business, be an outstanding General Manager, or an incredible sports person. It all comes down to the identity you create for yourself, the ceilings you place over yourself, how well you can visualise what it is you want to achieve, and your ability to make some changes.

Above all, if you want to steal back your Mojo, you need to let go of your old thinking. You have a lot more in common than you think with people such as Donald Trump, Richard Branson, Oprah Winfrey, Pete Sampras, Jack Nicklaus, Tiger Woods and other extraordinary individuals - you are just missing a Mojo mindset. Remember the only person who can steal your Mojo is yourself - and now it's time to steal it back by creating a Mojo mindset.

CLUELESS

I recently had the opportunity to speak in London alongside Sahar Hashemi, creator of the huge UK retail coffee brand Coffee Republic. During her presentation Sahar spoke of her passion for coffee, people and team-work. In her book *Anyone Can Do It*, Sahar Hashemi makes reference to one of her entrepreneurial philoso-phies, and that is being 'clueless'. Sahar also talks a lot about being clueless when she addresses audiences at conferences.

Sahar was a practising solicitor before leaving the legal profession to open up an American-style coffee bar in London. She openly admits she had little experi-ence in this industry, and went into the whole venture 'totally clueless'. I think this is a wonderful philosophy for people, particularly entrepreneurs, to carry with them - a feeling of being clueless.

Quite often what prevents us from taking on new challenges or opportunities is the desire to know all about what to do, when to do it, and what the outcomes are likely to be before we go into it. As Sahar says, you do need to do your due diligence, put together some sort of business plan, and have an idea in your own mind and ideally be able to visualise your outcomes, however at the same time she believes it is important to carry an element of cluelessness with you. This can be a wonderful way to stimulate your Mojo. Really, you don't need to know every detail in order to get started. As Sahar and her brother did with the Coffee Republic chain, you can learn as you go along.

Put another way, I once heard someone say, 'Don't let perfection stand in the way of a great idea.' This principle is along the same lines as the clueless mindset. In order to get your Mojo going, try to firstly visualise the idea, then gather as much information together as you possibly can, but don't worry if you don't know all the details or exactly how you're going to do it before you start.

Albert Einstein often said 'I don't know what I don't know', and I think this ties in nicely with the clueless philosophy. Einstein was continually frustrated when attending functions with other scientists as they would regularly talk about either what they knew or what they didn't know. Einstein believed that doing this was closing their minds to other possibilities. Even when he knew the answer to something, Einstein always made a point of asking a question, and this was his way of being clueless. Instead of being a know-all and having all the answers, Einstein chose to be clueless on purpose as he believed that by not knowing what you don't know, you inherently opened up your mind to all sorts of possibilities.

For me, creativity is about creating options. So if you believe in your own mind that you have all the answers, you are in effect shutting off the potential for new horizons and new options. Being clueless opens up that part of the brain that looks for the 'I don't know' angle. This is also particularly powerful when you're in conversation with others as it encourages you to ask more or better questions. Rather than going into conversations with friends, business partners or family and knowing it all, taking a clueless approach encourages you to ask more questions, be genuinely interested in the answers, and in the end be a more engaging and considerate participant in the conversation.

Naivety in the sense of being clueless can be a wonderful and powerful tool to stimulate your Mojo. It opens up better conversations, more possibilities, a greater sense of adventure, and the opportunity to make a start, rather than waiting for all the details before you take the first step. In the right context I think 'cluelessness' is a wonderful tool to help you steal back your Mojo.

DRILLING FOR IDEAS

What would it be like to have your own oil field? What would it be like to know that you owned an oil rig that if tapped, could open up a wealth of knowledge, ideas, profit and everything you'd ever dreamed of? What if that oil field was right in your own back yard? The point is, that it is!

While presenting at a conference in Austin, Texas, USA, I discussed the topic of drilling down for ideas with another presenter. Our discussion centred around the fact that quite often our thinking and solutions to problems is very shallow, almost reactionary, and in many cases the most logical answer. Most people when faced with a problem or an opportunity tend to go with the first idea that comes to mind. We base our decision making process on logic without drilling further for other possibilities. The metaphor that I have drawn with the oil field is based on the fact that generally, your best ideas will come from the last third of the ideas that you have.

For example, when having a creative session in your own mind or brainstorming with a group of people, your best ideas will come from the last third of the brainstorming concepts that you come up with. Why is that? It's because the last third are always the ones that come once you have already eliminated or thought past the logical ideas and you've started to ask 'what else?'.

The deeper you drill down into your creative mind, the more unusual and in most cases valuable, your ideas will be. You should never settle for your first idea. You need to constantly dig for more and better options. This is the true way to unlock your innate creative talent. Everybody has the ability to come up with ideas and those that find the most unique ideas or different ways of thinking are those that hang with their problems or opportunities the longest, in order to drill for the deepest ideas.

The challenge comes in getting people to hang in there long enough to be able to drill down below the surface and get to the really great ideas. Here are three tips for you to consider in order to drive your oil rig deeper to find those great ideas:

Take time. Have a look at your diary for today and the rest of the week, and if you haven't allocated time specifically to sit and ponder, then you haven't taken the time to open the shaft to your mind. In order to drill below the surface and find your real oil reserve of ideas you need to make time to think. As Leonardo Da Vinci once said 'a busy mind has no place for creativity'.

Break your habits. If you always do what you've always done, you'll always get what you've always got - and that simply may not be good enough. By doing things differently each day, you'll be stimulating your creative mind and digging for new and better ideas. From choosing somewhere different for lunch, reading a magazine on a topic you would never imagine reading, watching a documentary on a new book, going to work a different way, or buying a book on something you know nothing about, you will be stretching your mind and stimulating your thinking. A mind once stretched, never resumes its original shape.

Always think in terms of options. Never settle for your first answer and always push the boundaries of your creativity by creating more and more options. The more you ask yourself 'what else?', the more you will sink your oil rig deeper into your ideas reservoir. The longer you spend and the more questions you ask, the richer you are likely to become with the ideas that are brought to the surface.

You may think this sounds a bit simplistic, but in order to get down to your great ideas, it actually is that simple. Spend time, stimulate your mind, break your habits, and always look for more than one answer.

The thing for you to consider is that it's your right to drill as the rig is in *your* mind. Each person has this enormous reservoir of ideas, oil field, waiting to be tapped. It's your mind and it's your choice as to whether you choose to make use of your own creative ability. The thing that drives the drill down to bring your ideas to the surface is the thought of creating more and better options.

Creative thinking is something that each person is blessed with, it's not something that only a select few have. Everyone has the potential to do it, and the more you practice it the better you will get at coming up with ideas and solutions for problems. The thing with oil is that we know its down there, the challenge is bringing it to the surface and doing something with it. One last point to consider is that if you choose to take up the opportunity to drill for your own oil, while you're down there you may even strike gold in the process!

BE A BRAND

I spend a lot of time facilitating workshops for companies to assist them in developing a marketing plan.

We can spend hours deciding who the brand should be talking to, what the brand is about, and why the brand is different to it's competitors. Recently I got to thinking about how companies market their brands to consumers and realised that maybe it's time that people discussed a marketing plan for themselves.

My thought is that each one of us should consider ourselves to be a brand. Are you marketing yourself to those that you are responsible to? That is, the boss. If you are running a large company, then you may need to be marketing yourself to the Board. If you are the payroll officer of an organisation then you may need to be marketing yourself to your boss. Here are four steps to help you do this:

1. Work out who you need to promote yourself to.
2. Define what you do in one simple sentence that summarises your job.
3. Summarise why you are different and what makes you unique to anybody else who may have that job. (Try to summarise it in one word.)
4. How will you let people know? How will you demonstrate it or promote yourself to those above or around you?

The last one is an interesting question. If you are doing exactly the same job with no real point of difference or real skills or strengths over somebody else, then why do they need you? This is one of the most defining questions for any brand, why should the consumer pick you off the shelf and not your competitor?

One of the key things that I work on with my clients is finding one word which sums up why you are different and what you would like to come to mind when somebody thinks about your brand or product. In other words, when somebody thinks about you in your role, what one word would come to mind for them? For example, if you were going to buy a toothpaste today and you wanted to buy one that would fight cavities, which brand would you choose? That's right: Colgate! If you were going to buy a toothpaste because you wanted a great smile, which one would you choose? Correct again: Macleans. You see, each one has worked for many years to cement in your mind the one word they want to own. The questions for you are, what makes you different and what one word separates you from other people who may do a similar job?

Once you've answered these questions, the next question is, how will you tell your boss about it? Will you demonstrate it through meetings by coming in early, by being proactive with your ideas, by being on time, by being prompt, having suggestions in meetings and so on. There are a myriad of different ways in which you can promote yourself to your target. Now I know that a lot of people won't sit down with this model and put pen to paper to start marketing themselves. But if you take thirty seconds to think about these simple questions in your own mind, you might surprise yourself with how simple this really is, and what a difference you can make in the way you go about promoting yourself to those above or around you.

Marketing is not hard, and it's not only appropriate for the Coca-Colas and Telstras of the world (mind you they could do with some help too at times!). It is just as appropriate for you and I as individuals to start promoting ourselves to those around us as it is to those big brands trying to get you to choose their product.

One of my heroes of all time is P.T. Barnum, from Barnum and Bailey's Circuses. P.T. Barnum once said 'a terrible thing happens when you don't promote yourself . . . nothing'.

BE CURIOUS

In my first book *The Keys to Creativity*, I described the five traits of a creative thinker - confidence, persistence, time, courage and curiosity. Curiosity sparks Mojo. Creative types tend to be curious. They want to know what else can be done, how it can be done differently, what comes next, why it can't be done that way, or even who says? Curious people are the ones constantly asking the questions that create new ways of doing things. The curious mind is the one that builds Mojo by finding exciting new frontiers to explore and discovering ways of making things better.

Free thinkers and creative types ask better and different questions of themselves and others. They're always wondering about things, and asking questions such as 'What would happen if . . . ?' To get your Mojo working you need to ask more questions of yourself and those around you. The juice or the Mojo exists in the process of challenging and asking the right questions.

Creative thinkers are always looking for the next interesting thing to do. Perhaps that may be embarking on a holiday to a new destination, buying an unusual present for a friend, finding a unique book to read, or simply finding a different recipe for dinner. Creative thinkers are happy to experiment and are not deterred by failure, so if something doesn't work the first time they'll look to other possibilities and go from there.

You may recall the movie *Dead Poets Society* starring Robin Williams as a poetry teacher in an American boys college. In my favourite scene the teacher has the boys in the class stepping up onto the teacher's desk at the front of the study hall. Williams' character Keating encourages them to stand there for a moment and look around, and then he says:

I stand upon my desk to remind myself that we must constantly look at things in a different way . . . just when you think you know something, you have to look at it another way. Even though it may seem silly or wrong, you must try . . . Boys you must strive to find your own voice. Because the longer you wait to begin, the less likely you are to find it at all.

Don't be satisfied with only one way of doing things. Don't put up with mediocrity. Rather, find new, interesting and fun ways to do things. Albert Einstein has been quoted as saying that he did not believe he was that smart, but he did believe that he was passionately curious. Fuel your Mojo by fostering your creative curiosity.

This poem by Walter Wintle sums up the importance of a Mojo mindset:

THE MAN WHO THINKS HE CAN

If you think you are beaten you are;
If you think you dare not, you don't.
If you'd like to win, but you think you can't,
It's almost a cinch you won't.
If you think you'll lose, you've lost,
For out of the world we find
Success begins with a fellow's will;
It's all in the state of mind.
If you think you're outclassed, you are;
You've got to think high to rise.
You've got to be sure of yourself
Before you can ever win a prize.
Life's battles don't always go
To the stronger or faster man;
But sooner or later the man who wins
Is the one who thinks he can.

MOJO CHECK-UP

✓ Am I looking at all the options?
✓ Can I look at things differently?
✓ Am I taking 'me time' to ponder?
✓ Am I controlling the controllables?
✓ Am I getting out of my routine to stimulate my creative spirit?
✓ Have I fallen back into my old identity?
✓ Are there new words I need to eliminate from my vocabulary?

CHAPTER 2
RAISE THE ROOF

Late one evening after an athletics training session I was doing the cool down session with a running partner. My partner that night was Paul, winner of some of Australia's biggest and toughest road races and marathons. He had an impeccable record over long-distance running and was seen as one of Australia's finest.

As we ambled along engrossed in conversation, as was normally the case after we'd finished the hard work, I was asking Paul about his attitude towards training. He said he believed that athletics and performance was all in the mind. Although I tended to agree with him on some level, I did challenge him on that premise, given the fact that I had heard so much about the Africans and the advantage of their body structure, shape and tone. Although he agreed that was true to a certain extent, he also held his belief that running ability was largely in the mind. And once again I challenged him.

At that point Paul turned to me in stride and said, 'Gary, do you believe you can be the best in the world?' Anybody who knows me knows that a question such as this is like a red rag to a bull. What do you say to a question like that? Even if you said yes, in the back of your mind you'd be thinking to yourself, 'you're kidding'. Like you're going to be able to beat the Africans - the Tanzanians, the Moroccans. Yet, if you said no, it could be seen as a self-fulfilling prophecy, and therefore you're placing a limit on your ability.

The only thing I could think of was to say to Paul, 'I think I can achieve my goals.' At that point Paul looked me in the eye and repeated, 'Gary, do you think you can be the best in the world?' Once again there was dead silence for what seemed like an hour. We continued to run our cool down yet I still had no answer for Paul's question. I didn't want to say yes because I knew it wasn't true, yet in the back of my mind I knew if I said no, it would be a limiting belief. So consequently I did the only thing I felt I could do, and that was to take a turn in the road and go off on my own so I could ponder the question further.

For a full week I deliberated on an answer to Paul's question. Finally just before training the following week, I came up with a solution. I resolved to believe that if I approached every day like I was going to be the best in the world, then the rest would take care of itself. If I ate the right foods, did high-performance training sessions, had the right shoes, the right chiropractor, the right physio, and approached everything I did with the mental attitude that I was going to be the best in the world, my performance could go from X to X + 1. In other words, if I held myself to the standard of being the world's best and did what the world's best would do, would my performance go from X to X + 1?

That night I went back to training and had a long discussion with Paul about this approach. He said to me that for ten years he considered himself to be the best in the world, and his goal was to run a world-best time of two hours and eight minutes in the marathon. To this day Paul keeps getting closer and closer to his goal. Any outstanding performer sees themselves as being the best in their chosen field.

In a recent interview with an Australian television station, Sean Combs, otherwise known as P. Diddy, said that although he wasn't sure what field he'd eventually make it in he always knew he would be the best in the world at something. Although he doesn't think he's there yet, he keeps on pushing himself. And judging by the line up of performers he is producing for, the number of CDs he's sold, and the amount of clothes he is moving through his fashion label, you'd have to agree that this mindset has certainly been an asset to P. Diddy!

So back to the running. After my discussion with Paul I started to approach my running differently, and funnily enough I started to see changes in my performance. Within a week, where previously I would have finished at the back of the pack in a sprint session, I was finishing middle of the pack and even towards the front. Suddenly guys who had been beating me by 20 metres in a 400 metre session were now finishing behind me. It seemed that almost immediately things started to change for me. I started to approach my training, my nutrition, my rests and mental attitude completely differently.

Two weeks later we lined up at the Australian Half Marathon championships in Sydney. My mindset on this day was not to line up hoping to finish in the top ten per cent, but to believe that I could win my age group, and that the other athletes would be chasing me. It was a hard day and a tough course, but I managed to take four minutes off my personal best and finish just 20 seconds behind the winner of my age group.

To this day I still remember crossing the line and thinking to myself, 'What happened?' What was so dramatically different that in one month of training I could suddenly go from finishing in the top ten per cent to finishing just 20 seconds from winning the title for my age group in the Australian championship and taking a massive four minutes off my personal best?

The following week I read a quote in a magazine that said, 'One man's ceiling is another man's floor.' I suddenly realised that I had been placing ceilings over myself in many aspects of my world for too many years. I had created a ceiling that was preventing me from finishing a book that I had been writing for three-and-a-half years. I'd even created a ceiling over having a baby because I was concerned about being a good dad, and what it would be like having a child. I created ceilings in my speaking career, in my athletics, and in my home life. I'd always seen myself as being good at things, but never great or outstanding. I'd created ceilings over myself that had prevented me from being the best I could be in my life.

People who do a good job get okay results. In every organisation there are people who do a great job who end up getting the very good results. But in any given field, no matter what it is, there is always one person who is outstanding, and it is the people who are outstanding that get the great results. This diagram sums up my approach to raising the roof.

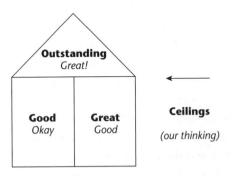

In any given room that I stand in front of in my speeches, whether it be ten or a hundred people, whenever I ask for a volunteer there's always one person who'll be first to put their hand up. There's always one person who wants to go longer and harder and be better than they are. While in some sessions some people will be tired at five o'clock in the afternoon, there will always be one person who says, 'No let's just do a bit more and get this job done.' There's always someone who wants more in some aspect of their life.

The difference between a great person and an outstanding person is not skills, it is simply a difference in desire, or as Vince Lombardi (the famous Green Bay Packers coach in the American NFL) said, 'The difference between a successful person and others, it's not a lack of strength, not a lack of knowledge, but rather a lack of will.' Many times, if not all of the time, the difference will just be that the person who is outstanding wants to stand out and is prepared to do whatever it takes in order to achieve that.

I realised through my running that I had not held myself to a high enough standard, and through the things that I was saying to myself in my own mind I was creating ceilings over my potential. Having removed those ceilings, during the following year I finished the book, gained a national distributor, and received fantastic support from bookshops. I also had a beautiful, healthy baby girl, achieved excellent results with my athletics, and started to reap the rewards of holding myself to a standard of outstanding.

There is no Mojo to be found in being bland or mediocre. But from my experience when you start to hold yourself to a standard of outstanding, you start to surprise yourself with the results you can achieve, and it certainly spurs your Mojo.

Raising the roof is not about bragging or spruiking that you are the best, it's just an inner knowledge in your own heart and mind that sets the bar higher than mediocre, higher than bland, and higher than those around you. It is an internal spark that when fuelled turns into a raging flame. It by no means requires you to wave a flag and boast and brag or act with arrogance towards those around you. Sometimes raising the roof and being outstanding is misunderstood and misconstrued as being arrogant, and it's normally by those who are holding themselves to a standard of mediocre.

There comes a time in many people's lives when they want more. They want more from their interests, from their job, and from all aspects of their life. This is when people start to push mediocrity aside and hold themselves to a standard of outstanding. The sad thing for most people is that being outstanding sounds like a lot of hard work, but it's not. It's just a change of thinking and holding yourself to a position where you're not satisfied being ordinary. Ordinary people are doing extraordinary things every day, and this comes from changing their thinking, raising the roof and holding themselves to a higher standard. If you're coasting along just doing your job, why not try to see if you can be more and do more, and as a result see how much more you get in return.

THE WORKOUT

When you're at the gym and working out on a set of weights, most people will do ten repetitions in each set. When doing those ten repetitions, which one hurts the most? Of course it's number ten. But which one do you get the most value from? That's right, number eleven! Why is it that ten is the magic number assumed by visitors to the gym and, more importantly, personal trainers throughout the world? It seems everyone is fixated with doing ten repetitions. Which is fine for them . . . but remember you're not like everyone else. In order to raise the roof you must push beyond this barrier of ten and look to do eleven or more. If you're simply content being one of the crowd, then by all means, continue doing ten. However, if you in fact want to be outstanding, then you will need to push yourself past everyone else and do eleven or more.

I constantly see personal trainers in gyms encouraging their clients to reach the magic mark of ten, pushing them through seven, eight, nine . . . and just one more . . . *ten*. This is in fact creating a subconscious barrier, not only for weights but everything we do. Especially given that only a small percentage of clients will push past that barrier of their own will, and want more, expect more, do more and deliver more.

While training for the Boston marathon, my coach would have us run a sprint session each Tuesday night. The sprint session was repetitions of 300 metres, 400 metres, 600 metres and 800 metres. Invariably when he set us a task of twelve repetitions of 400 metres in an evening, the majority of the squad would hold themselves back until number ten and eleven, until finally for number twelve they would give it all they have and then cross the finish line exhausted and spent.

Knowing what it took to run marathons, my coach would then say, 'Great session guys, let's just do one more.' It always staggered me that the last repetition, number thirteen, would always have us producing times that were either equal to or better than any other repetitions that night. He knew that we always had one more set in us, and he knew that as outstanding athletes we needed to push ourselves further than our opponents who were doing a similar track session on another track somewhere else in the world. He also knew that at the 35-kilometre mark in a marathon when it really starts to hurt, the extra work we'd done would hold us in good stead.

This concept can even be applied to your preparation for meetings, being an outstanding parent, the thought you put into weekends or special occasions, right through to your commitment to a school committee or your local touch football club. Rather than doing just what's expected, you need to raise the roof and deliver plus one. Rather than satisfying the customers - delight them. Look at what is expected and then over-deliver. I once heard a great saying, 'Overpromise and over-deliver'.

I think the gym analogy is a great metaphor for raising the roof and fuelling your Mojo. People with Mojo seem to want, deliver and be more than those without it. If you would like to prove this fact to yourself, next time you go to the gym, watch the robots all doing ten repetitions in a set. And then think to yourself that you're not like everyone else.

LiVE LiKE YOU ARE DYiNG

Early one morning when I was out with my cycling buddies we came around a bend and saw the most incredible view of the coastline. Our group slowed to a halt, and made various comments about the incredible sight before us. It made me think, do most people really live or are we only just existing? My belief is that a lot of people are going through the motions, doing the same things day in day out, yet complaining because they're not getting the most out of life. In other words, they have lost their Mojo.

Hollywood heart-throb and leading man Matthew McConaughey promoted a film called *Sahara* a year or two ago. The manner in which he went about promoting the movie across America was unique and hence the basis for a documentary. McConaughey painted a large Airstream caravan as the insignia for the movie, then towed it behind a pickup, and travelled across the centre of America. Along the way he stopped to promote the film in many small American townships, and instead of staying in the five-star hotels that you would expect from most movie stars, he parked the Airstream in local caravan parks and hung out with the locals. I found the documentary fascinating and just as interesting as Matthew.

Matthew McConaughey's attitude to his life and how he does things is a great example of someone who has Mojo. His production company is called simply j.k. livin' - 'j' for just and 'k' for keep. His philosophy is that life is about living and every day is about doing whatever you can to live it to the max. Exercise and health are very important to him, but instead of working out in the gym, he runs along unusual trails and fire paths he finds in forests, and also does exercises using his natural body weight out in the open countryside. He's an adventurer and that's how he approaches his life.

American country singer Tim McGraw won many awards - including Song of the Year in 2004 at the

Country Music Awards - for his hit song *Live Like You Were Dying*. The lyrics tell the story of a guy who found out that he had only a short time to live and how this prompted him to go climbing in the Rockies, bucking a bull, and having a different relationship with those around him. The chorus is, 'Some day I hope you get the chance to live like you were dying.' Live now, as though you were dying.

Have a think to yourself; are you really living your life or are you just existing? Do you merely endeavour to just make it through every day or are you making every day count? The sad thing is that when most people finish on this planet, they will more than likely look back with regret over things they have not done. Take a minute and have a think to yourself now. Will you look back and say, 'That was a brilliant life, I did everything I wanted to do and lived it just the way I wanted to live it?' If you're in doubt as to what you'd say if you reached that point and had to look back now, thankfully it's not too late.

MAY i TAKE YOUR BAGS?

On one of my trips to Melbourne I stayed at the Westin Hotel in the centre of the city. This is one of my favourite hotels anywhere in the world. I often think about my first visit to this hotel some time back. When I pulled up in a taxi the concierge opened my door, and while I paid for the taxi he asked how many bags I had in the back. As I only had a small bag, I said, 'Just one, thank you.' The concierge came around to the side of the car and said, 'I'll take your bag to your room for you Mr Bertwistle.' At first I was a bit concerned, until I realised he'd been very efficient and seen my name on the tag on my suitcase. While I sat there waiting for my taxi driver to process my credit card payment, the concierge opened the lobby door to allow guests in and out of the hotel on three separate occasions. He was totally aware of what was going on around him and made sure he kept an eye on my progress. Once the taxi driver finally gave me my receipt, the concierge closed the door to the taxi and gave me a small business card. On the business card was the name of four different taxi companies, with a tick next to the one I had just used. Not only was it ticked it also had the actual number of the taxi. The concierge then said to me, 'Welcome to the Westin Hotel Mr Bertwistle. If you've left anything in the taxi I've got the name and number of the cab here, so we can give them a quick call to collect whatever you've left. My name is John; have an excellent stay.'

John was by far the most professional and most proficient concierge I've ever come across at any hotel, anywhere in the world. He was simply outstanding, and from that moment the tone had been set for me at the Westin Hotel.

There is not a lot of difference in the effort required to be good, great or outstanding. All it takes is discipline and some new thinking. John, in a simple two-minute introduction to the hotel, demonstrated both these things. Consider the small things you can do that will take you from doing a good job to a great job or an outstanding job. There are good concierges, and I've even met some great ones, but the way that John treated me in that first meeting elevated him to outstanding.

Outstanding is a way of thinking, a discipline, and it's holding yourself to a standard that's higher than anyone else could possibly hold you to. That's the trick to outstanding service and outstanding results. I'm surprised at how many people simply cruise through life quite happy to be good at what they do and receiving good or average results.

If you see yourself as being okay or average, then that's exactly what you're going to get. If you see yourself as being outstanding then that's also what you'll deliver. You need to act the way you want to become until you become the way you act. If you want to be the best then you need to hold yourself to that standard. It's amazing how just by raising the roof and holding yourself to the standard of the best, you can change your identity and hence change the results that you receive. This has been proven time and time again by sportspeople, businesspeople, authors and everyday people who suddenly realise they have more talent and ability than they gave themselves credit for, but once they realise it, the results speak for themselves.

When the world tragically lost the Crocodile Hunter Steve Irwin it was a shock for millions of people. Steve unquestionably had tons of Mojo. In a television interview with the Channel 9 network in Australia, his wife Terri spoke glowingly about her hero, Steve. One of the things she mentioned during the interview was how Steve would always encourage her to be better than she was. In fact, he had a way of encouraging everyone around him to be their best. He could always see that people were capable of far more than they gave themselves credit for, and he had the ability to draw it out of them.

One of my favourite movies is *Any Given Sunday* with Al Pacino, who plays the burnt-out coach of a Miami NFL team. In one of the last matches of the season Pacino's character tells his team, 'Life is a game of inches . . . the inches we need are all around us, and we will fight for that inch . . . because we know when we add them up, that's what's going to make the difference.' It's the guy who's prepared to go the extra inch who will get the greatest rewards. Raising the roof is about doing the small things that make all the difference. When you start doing this and you start surprising yourself with the results and people start to acknowledge you and ask you how you do it, it fires your Mojo. The other important thing is not to let other people's opinions, their beliefs or their words get into your head and create ceilings for you that will hold you back from being your best. That will definitely steal your Mojo.

SOMETHING TO BE PROUD OF

In 2005, I was scheduled to run the New York Marathon. Unfortunately due to a cartilage injury in my right knee I was deemed unable to run. However, because the airfares and accommodation had already been booked, I decided to take my wife on a holiday to New York and support a running buddy of mine who was competing in the race. Because I wasn't able to run at all, I was restricted to training each day in the swimming pool or on the bike.

The afternoon before the race I was doing a session on the bike and listening to a song called *Something to be Proud Of* by a terrific American country band called Montgomery Gentry. The lyrics talk about a grandad bringing up his son to realise that it's the things going on in his life apart from work that were the things to be most proud of. So it got me thinking about the things I am most proud of in my life. Some of the smallest things that up until now I'd thought insignificant were actually the moments or events that could make me most proud. When you stop and take a moment to list some of the things you are proud of it can be quite emotional. It can also be quite surprising. In this day and age, people are so busy ploughing ahead and just getting the job done, we sometimes don't sit back and take stock and think about some of the things we're proud of. Those things can be anything from family and friends to achievements and goals, and so on.

My buddy who raced in the New York Marathon ended up running about 30 minutes slower than he had anticipated. Where he thought he would run a personal best and potentially win a place in his age group and in the race, like a lot of runners he hit the wall just after half way and struggled home in a way that made him feel quite disappointed. Being a champion Australian runner and venturing all the way to New York only to not run a PB as expected can be quite disheartening. I had breakfast with him the morning after the race, and with the *Something to be Proud Of* thought in the back of my mind we talked about the fact that just being able to get into the sub-elite category in the New York Marathon was something to be proud of. The fact that his wife, sister and other family members were there to watch him race in such a big global event was also something to be proud of. After our discussion, he went away and set some new targets and goals for the summer track sessions ahead back home in Australia.

It is important to take time to step back and think about the things that we have accomplished and that make us proud. The people who love us, the difference we've made in the lives of others, the donations we've made in one way or another, or the way we've contributed to someone else feeling good, better or different about themselves.

When you sit down and list some of the things that you are most proud of, it can help you generate your Mojo for the future. Sometimes it even makes you appreciate that life is not as tough or as hard as we imagine, and there are some great things going on that we just haven't taken the time to acknowledge. Some of the things we see as being most insignificant are quite often the things that we should be most proud of.

Hopefully after reading this you will sit down with your journal and list some of the things that you are most proud of. Don't leave anything out as it is your list and is always something you can fall back on when you want to steal back your Mojo. Journaling can be such a wonderful tool as a way of reigniting your Mojo.

I once met a real estate agent who was considered to be one of the finest in Sydney, who told me that he always kept thankyou letters from people he had helped with real estate. He said that real estate goes through peaks and troughs, and that sometimes during the troughs, everything can feel like doom and gloom. If ever he felt his Mojo slipping away he would pull open his folder and read the letters that made him acknowledge the things he should be proud of, and reignited his Mojo in order to get through the tough times.

INFO

We live in the information age and on a daily basis we are surrounded by new information, new findings and different nuggets of wisdom. It constantly surprises me how rarely people record these facts, especially given that the majority of people learn visually; that is, through seeing something. It's also been proven that repetition is one of the greatest assets we have for learning, yet most of us hear or see something once, and don't record it. If people expect to hear or see something once and remember it, they're kidding themselves. For me, the majority of our new ideas are like birds in a tree. You admire them while you can see them, but as soon as you turn your back the bird is gone forever, and indeed so are our ideas. While they are in the front of our minds we admire them, but as soon as we turn our attention to something else, the idea is gone, in most cases never to be seen again.

As I sit on planes, buses and in presentations, I constantly see people absorbing information from lectures, conferences, books and audio programs, without writing a single thing down. Often I find myself sitting in meetings with executives where we share information but they do not take one single note. It's frightening to think of how many good ideas are going in one ear and out the other. What is truly amazing is that these people expect to remember what they've heard, even though it's been proven that only one in ten people learn simply by hearing. Auditory learners are the smallest percentage of learners in society.

Every day there are loads of sayings, learnings, bits of information, motivating pieces and gems of wisdom that could be recorded and used, not only now but in the future. My suggestion is to find yourself a good journal or notebook that you can carry with you at all times, and whenever you hear a great quote, a new piece of information, a technique or a tool, make a note of it. When you're reading a book, always carry a highlighting pen or a pencil. If you don't, you're letting an opportunity slip away.

To be better tomorrow than you are today you need to learn new information and techniques, either from those you meet, things you read or stuff you hear and see. A new piece of information, a stimulating quote or a gem of wisdom may be just what you need to steal back your Mojo, and having a journal full of all this information could be the ideal resource for you to visit whenever you feel your Mojo is being stolen away or you just need a pep up.

A week or so after I finish reading a book I go back to it, take out all the pieces I have highlighted and write them into my journal. I find the repetition of seeing a piece of information, highlighting it, going back and re-reading the highlights, entering them into my journal and then re-reading them helps me remember what I've learned. Most books these days cost £9 or £10, and I want to make sure I get my money's worth. I also pass a lot of the information I learn onto others through speeches, presentations and one-on-one sessions, as well as sharing information with my friends and family, in order to help them be the best they can be.

When you keep a journal full of great notes you have collected each day it becomes your ultimate encyclopedia for self-development, self-help and motivation. Aristotle said, 'Man is born with a thirst for knowledge.' It's what you hear, see and feel that feeds that thirst. But it's your pen and paper that are your utensils. Use them well and feed your thirst and be better for it. Create your own Mojo encyclopedia. Buy a journal today!

GET ORGANISED

People with Mojo are calm, organised and have time to get things done. There's no place for Mojo in a stressed, busy and out-of-control life. Have you ever worked with somebody who always has a plan to follow for everything they do? These people always have contingency plans for 'what ifs' and 'just in case' scenarios. People with Mojo tend to ask lots of questions about what's going on, what's happening, or what could be. They also seem to have the time to complete everything they want to do. For them, everything has to be done in a certain way, according to their plan, and within a certain time frame. They have the whole thing mapped out before it even takes place. They also have all the information they need in order to do something, before they do it, enabling them to make quick decisions.

One of the keys to stealing back your Mojo is stealing back your time. We live in an age of multitasking. Most people seem to live their lives in a busy, confused, stressed and time-poor manner. In order to be able to steal back your Mojo, you need to have the time to do it, and in order to make this time you need to make better choices about how you use the time that you have.

I'm not a great believer in time management, as I don't think you actually can manage time. Mother nature has its own agenda and there's nothing you can say or do that can change how time progresses. The only thing you *can* control is how you go about using the time that you have, and getting organised is one of the most important elements when choosing how to use your time more efficiently.

Some time ago a tip was shared with me that has made immeasurable difference to my world. Each night before I finish my day, I plan what needs to be done tomorrow. Now this is something that is not uncommon in most planning. But what was suggested to me was that when you're planning for the following day, outline all the things you'd like to get done and then mark the top six. These are the six critical and imperative things that you need to have done in order for it to be a productive day, even if you are not able to complete anything else. The other tip that was suggested to me was to start the day with the thing that you least look forward to.

By doing this, you not only get immense satisfaction out of knowing that the hard one is done and out of the way, it also means that you are left with the easier or more enjoyable tasks. This tool has served me well for many years, and I have also received a lot of positive feedback from others who have tried it. The other advantage is that it allows you to determine what the important and not-so important tasks are in any given day, and it gives you the opportunity to focus on the important ones first in order to get them ticked off your list.

To have your Mojo working you have to be calm and have time to think in order to get things done, and this does mean getting somewhat organised. The top six idea is a terrific tool that you can use to prioritise what needs to be done and when it needs to be done by, and in doing so you'll also get yourself organised, giving yourself more time to steal back your Mojo.

One little note on the side of this is, don't think that the top six have to all be about work. People tend to have written goals and be extremely organised inside the workplace, but when it comes to outside the office, where Mojo is also important, those goals are often put on the back burner. Make sure that amongst your top six you have some time allocated for play, family or social activity, as this too will help stimulate and foster your Mojo.

I have always been a great advocate of goal writing, as I truly believe that written goals have a much greater likelihood of coming true than those that are simply spinning around in your head. When I first left the corporate world to work for myself, I was sitting in a seminar and the presenter asked me to write down in the back of my journal the goals that I had set for myself for two, five and ten years time. He said that we don't need to visit the goals on a daily basis, but just check-in every couple of months to see how they're going. So I was surprised some years later when I went back to my journal and looked over the goals I'd written down, to find that I had actually achieved 75 per cent of them. How it happened I'm not sure, but I can assure you that once goals are written down, they seem to have an incredible way of coming true.

Goals that are floating around inside your mind are just dreams without a deadline. A Harvard University study found that only three per cent of new graduates had written goals. Ten years later the researchers interviewed the same graduates again, and found that the three per cent with written goals had accumulated more success and wealth than the other 97 per cent put together.

From my experience in speaking with hundreds of corporations and thousands of people, I'd have to say that those who have written goals are putting themselves way ahead of those who don't.

We also need to make sure that a few of our goals are lofty dreams. Most people only write down goals that they think they are likely to achieve, but all they're doing is placing a ceiling over their dreams and desires. Unfortunately most of us have been conditioned to think small and worry about the tall poppy syndrome. But as Nelson Mandela said, 'There is no passion to be found in playing small - in settling for a life that is less than the one you are capable of living.' Dream big, think big, and the law of attraction will work its magic to take you towards those goals. Having said that, you do need to work every day towards achieving those goals and that's where the top six concept provides enormous value.

Sam Walton, founder of the world's largest retail chain, American-based Walmart, was a great believer in goals. He said, 'Develop goals so that they are out of reach, but not so that they are out of sight.' He loved to stretch himself and others to be their best.

ESCAPE THE EVERYDAY, EVERY DAY

There's no doubt that when you return from holidays, you come back with that magical feeling that gets the Mojo fired up, and you feeling good. I'm sure everybody can relate to that wonderful feeling. You've had maybe two or three weeks away from the everyday and you come home feeling a million dollars. Sometimes you're tanned, you're definitely relaxed, and you're focused without a care in the world. However, within a few days of being back at work, the roof caves in and you're back to feeling exactly how you did before you went away. At this point you think - who stole my Mojo? Why can't we always feel like we have our Mojo going the way we do when we get back from a holiday? Why is it that we need to have two or three weeks away from the everyday in order to feel human again and steal back our Mojo?

Here are a few strategies that I've seen employed by people who in my opinion have their Mojo working:

Start the weekend early. I once worked with a guy who went into work an hour or two early on Fridays and consequently left an hour or two early in the afternoon. During the summer he spent a good hour to an hour-and-a-half on the beach on Friday afternoons, which made him feel like he was having a three-day weekend.

Pick something you love doing and get to it early on a Friday afternoon. Ideally get to it before the sun goes down. Whether it's catching up with a friend for a drink, seeing a movie, going shopping, or sitting in the park reading a book, when you do something that you love on a Friday afternoon, it certainly makes you feel like you've got an early start on the weekend. Try and do something that is outdoors in the sunlight and fresh air, but also something you feel passionate about.

Dedicate some time for reading on the weekend. It's common to hear people return from holidays discussing a book or two they have read while they've been away. However, once they fall back into the routine of their normal working week, the reading seems to go out the door along with their Mojo. So, this weekend grab a freshly brewed coffee or a pot of tea, find a tree and relax and immerse yourself in a book.

It's amazing how having an hour or two on the couch indulging in a good book can make you feel like new. This 'me time' is essential not only for relaxation but also for the stimulation it gives your creative mind. A great book is certainly a way of getting not only your spirit back, but also giving your Mojo an opportunity to work its magic.

Take a nap. One thing that happens when we're on holidays is that we take time to rest at any time of the day. Why is that? Because we can! When we're on holidays we don't feel guilty about having a snooze during the afternoon. So why should a normal week be any different? My suggestion is to not only get a good night's sleep a few nights a week - that is, be in bed by 8.30 or 9.00 o'clock in the evening - but also on the weekend try to catch a nap in the afternoon. It does wonders for your body, your spirit and your clarity of thought. It also makes you feel like the weekend is a short holiday. When not on holiday, we tend to fall back into the routine of the working week and conform to what the rest of society thinks should be done on a weekend. An afternoon nap is a chance to recharge the batteries, catch up on some of the sleep and rest you may have missed during the week, and it also gets your Mojo fired up for the rest of the weekend, setting you up for a great week ahead. It really is a wonderful indulgence that makes you look and feel terrific!

Eat well. There's been a lot said in magazines, books and newspapers about diet, but it's amazing how few of us are taking heed. When we return from holidays we generally look and feel terrific. Why is that? We're rested, we're relaxed, and we tend to eat better, healthier, and less often. This not only builds your immune system, but it increases your clarity of thought and boosts your spirit, giving you more energy to do the things you want to do. It brings back your Mojo.

It's not about diets so much as changing the way that you eat. As we discussed earlier, cut back on carbs, fat, sugar, alcohol and junk food. This will give you a lot more energy, and once again you will feel like you are on holiday. I'm sure at one time or another you have had a morning where you've left the house with a spring in your step and a glint in your eye and you just knew your Mojo is working. Guaranteed, you can trace that back to the rest that you've had, what you've done to stimulate your mind, and the food you've eaten. When these three pieces are aligned, that is when your Mojo works, which also means you don't *have* to go on holidays to feel like your Mojo is intact.

Meet new people. When we're on holiday and feel relaxed we seem to be more comfortable meeting and talking to new people. So, whether it's at a bar, on the beach or at a party, why not try to make a point of shaking hands with new people? Meeting new people can also bring back Mojo.

Sometimes an interesting conversation where you just relax and learn something new can leave you with a whole new approach to both your own world and the world around you. It could be a compliment from a stranger or even an invigorating discussion that leaves you feeling great. You may have recently thought about taking up a new sport or hobby or changing the direction of your life. You'd be surprised at how talking to new people can bring these things into your world and make them a reality. Once you have a goal in mind the laws of attraction seem to bring the right people to you at the right time in order to help you achieve your goals. You'd be amazed at what happens when you put your thoughts out there!

New scenery. When you are on holiday your senses are constantly stimulated by your new environment. Holidays break up your routine and you are happily forced to experience a new schedule, new scenery, different people and activities. Why not play foreigner in your own town? Take the long way home today and explore the back streets of your neighbourhood or city. Better yet, put on your walking shoes and walk the neighbouring suburbs or some different parts of your city. I love watching the sunset, and quite often seek out different parts of the city I'm visiting to watch the sunset. How can you not feel like you're on holiday when you're in a different environment, with different scenery, experiencing the spirit of a great sunrise or sunset? Why not hop out of bed a bit earlier than usual and watch the sun come up from a good vantage point in your city? Go to a different place for lunch, order something you've never had before, or take your lunch to a different corner of the local park near your office. Borrow some CDs from a friend, or channel flick on your radio at work for some new sounds. On the weekend, take a drive over a bridge, or go for a picnic to a place you've never been to before. Being in holiday mode could be as simple as going to a different beach or running on a different track to the one you would normally navigate. This will certainly help to spark the spirit of your Mojo, and you never know who you might meet along the way!

Do that thing you've always wanted to do - today. When you're on holiday you are more likely to try scuba diving or parasailing, climb a mountain or take a cooking class, or even try belly dancing. Why wait till you are halfway around the world to achieve one of these goals? Nothing gets the Mojo going more than when you stretch yourself into uncharted territory. This weekend seize the day and take on one of those things you've always wanted to do. I guarantee that on Monday morning you'll feel your Mojo working. Sure, you may need to make a few calls, do some research or book ahead, but the internet or your local telephone directory will easily take you towards your goal of a salsa class, sky dive or swimming with dolphins. Keep in mind that the things you've always wanted to do need not necessarily stretch you too far. It could even be as simple as going to a restaurant you've always wanted to go to with your parents for lunch. The important thing is to not wait to do things you've always wanted to - do them now, as there may not be a tomorrow.

So now you have some pointers you can use to make the most out of every day and to get away from the everyday.

Why wait for holidays to feel relaxed, less stressed, clearheaded, stimulated, and to get your Mojo working? Start today to take on one of these strategies, and watch your Mojo take off!

PARiS

One of the things I love about my job is that I get to travel to interesting cities around the world. However, like most executives I often find myself flying in early in the morning or late at night, doing what has to be done, getting back on the plane and flying home.

On a recent trip to London I chose to fly in a few days early, meet up with my brother in London and travel by train to Paris. We arrived in Paris early on a Saturday morning, and after dropping our bags at the club where we were staying, we spent the day strolling through the streets, heading in and out of cafes full of food and coffee. After a busy day on our feet, we headed back to the club, changed, and then went out to dinner. The next morning after breakfast we did the same thing, exploring the Parisian streets, going from cafe to cafe. Needless to say by the time we got back on the train to London on Sunday night we were both ready to spend a few hours sitting down.

On the return trip, my brother and I discussed what a great weekend we'd had and how what had only been less than 48 hours seemed like four or five days. It was quite interesting that even though we'd only arrived the morning prior it did seem as though we'd been away for a long time. We both agreed that because we'd spent our time exploring a new place with a new culture in completely different surroundings, it stimulated our minds in such a way that it made us feel as though we'd been away a lot longer.

I'm certainly not suggesting that you need to head to a European city every weekend in order to freshen up your mind and rejuvenate your Mojo! Maybe there's an interesting country town near where you live, maybe it's staying in a hotel on the other side of the city in which you live, or going to visit a friend in a city or town you've never been to. There's no doubt that breaking your routine and getting away from your familiar surroundings is a great way to spark and stimulate your Mojo.

Quite often we are so caught up in day-to-day life that we forget just how revitalising a break from the everyday can be, and consequently we don't get around to it. So my suggestion would be that every one, two or three months, schedule a weekend where you go exploring. Whether it's in the car, on the train or by plane, choose a destination that is within your budget and head out for the weekend. Leave your mobile phone, your Blackberry or your laptop at home and go and explore. Put on a backpack and seek out a great coffee or lunch or a wonderful antique or fashion store. Not only will this stimulate your Mojo but it's also a terrific way of engaging your creativity and imagination. New stimulation is a great way to have your mind break the habitual routine of Monday to Friday.

STRETCH

Poet T.S. Eliot once said, 'If you aren't in over your head, how do you know how tall you are?' It's surprising how many people live safely within their comfort zone. By moving outside your comfort zone you will give your Mojo a much needed kick along. Nothing gets the Mojo going like a shot of adrenalin or the feeling of knowing you have done something you weren't entirely sure you would be able to. Now this doesn't mean that you need to jump out of a plane or abseil down the side of a cliff, but my suggestion is that you think about some of the things that scare you a little or make you feel uncomfortable with the thought of stepping out of your comfort zone.

I saw a terrific speaker at a conference once who said that when somebody approaches him with an opportunity, if his initial reaction is that he shouldn't do it, then in his mind he knows has to. If it scares him then he's got to do it. He knows it's the things that scare him and challenge him the most that will draw him out of his comfort zone and invariably get his Mojo going.

Some of the greatest and most exhilarating moments that I've had in my working and personal life have come when I have taken on opportunities that at the time seemed a little beyond my ability. Quite often in my work when I've been asked to give a speech, the ones that have made me the most nervous or have forced me to step out of my comfort zone are the most rewarding and the ones that really get the blood pumping. And they are also the ones that, once completed, I look back on with the fondest memories.

Sometimes you need to stretch in order to steal back your Mojo. I like to say that these things that stretch you can be anything from 'mild' to 'wild'. Mild things are like that phone call to someone that you've been putting off or painting your bedroom an outrageous colour, to wild things like swimming with sharks, bungee jumping or diving into the freezing cold ocean on a winter morning.

The reason this is so important is because we've grown quite soft, comfortable and predictable in our lives. Many people I meet are stuck in a rut of blandness and mediocrity, trapped in routines and absorbed by the burdens of daily life. By stretching and finding an area that you can move into, an area of uncomfortableness, you can start to break this barrier of bland. Eleanor Roosevelt once said, 'you gain strength, courage and confidence through every experience in which you really stop to look fear in the face'. You must do the things you think you cannot do. The more times you push yourself past that barrier of discomfort, the more you will believe that the barrier is both moveable and passable. You will also find that the more you do it, the more you will get to like it and the more it will spur your Mojo.

I've always been a cowboy at heart and really admire the cowboy spirit. One day while out with a bunch of mates I happened to mention that I had always wanted to ride a bull. Completely out of the blue, one of the guys said, 'I can make it happen.' I knew that if I thought too much about it I'd back out, so I said, 'Great, let's go.'

Two months later the trip was organised and before I knew it the plane was landing in Rockhampton in central Queensland. That afternoon we went down to the chutes and loaded in a number of bulls ready for bucking out. The cowboys kitted me out in all the appropriate gear and took me through the ritual of stretching before getting on the back of the bull. The lead cowboy walked up to me and a bunch of other guys who were about to buck out, and asked us who wanted to go first. I don't even remember thinking about it before sticking my hand up and stepping forward. Within minutes I was sitting on the back of the bull being taken through all the necessary precautions before the chute opened.

I'd have to say that those three seconds that I spent on the back of a bull called Mac were some of the most exhilarating seconds of my life. At that point a lot of things changed for me, and I knew that the adrenalin and excitement of that short exercise certainly had started my Mojo going.

For months afterwards I would re-live the experience of being on the back of Mac. Once the bruising and soreness had gone away, I enjoyed it even more! I've since bucked out a number of bulls, and every time I jump on the back of one I feel the same sensation. But the sensation doesn't stop there. I've since been able to replicate it in lots of different areas of my life, from mild to wild.

This chapter is not about having to buck bulls or swim with sharks or do something else that is dangerous or exhilarating in that way. You certainly can, but what I'm saying to you is that Mojo happens when you get uncomfortable and surprise yourself by doing something you didn't think you were capable of.

There is amazing feeling, excitement, adrenalin rush and genuine happiness that comes from achieving something for the very first time. So, another question to ask yourself is when was the last time you did something for the first time? If your answer is 'not for a while', then sit down and consider what you could do this weekend for the very first time. Whether it's putting together some Ikea furniture, playing a new sport, exploring a new part of town, visiting a new restaurant, or redesigning your bedroom - it really doesn't matter what it is you do for the first time, it seems to have a remarkable effect on your state of mind and energy. It can also be something that you share with someone else. When you are motivated to attempt something for the first time, you'll often find that a friend is happy to do it with you, and this can help lessen any discomfort or nervousness you may be feeling.

Now if doing something for the first time is making you feel uncomfortable or stretched, then think about this line in the movie *Ronin* starring Robert De Niro, 'When there's doubt there is no doubt.' The more you do something, the more you get comfortable with being uncomfortable, and hence your Mojo grows. It could be as simple as stepping up to sing in front of a crowd at karaoke, taking yourself and your partner to a very expensive restaurant against all better judgement, or stripping off and swimming in a freezing ocean in the middle of winter. What you do and how you do it is entirely up to you, but if you want to get your Mojo working this is sure to ignite the flame.

A brilliant book on this topic is *NOW - No Opportunity Wasted* by Phil Keoghan, who is the host of the very successful global television show *The Amazing Race*. Phil describes how he nearly lost his life and realised he needed to do all those things that he'd been putting off. Phil takes you step by step through how to make a list of things to do before you die. It really is a great read and is a book that you won't regret having in your library.

People learn to live with disappointment because it's familiar and safe, but only by taking a risk can they accomplish the extraordinary. These same people who say 'can't' often really mean 'won't'. It's a matter of 'will'.

A WEALTH OF THiNKiNG

One of the greatest stresses that most of us face is concern about our finances. In the past few years, I have had both staff members and people I've worked with come to me for advice about their financial situations. I have taken a great interest in the psychology of money in the last fifteen years, and as a result it has helped me to build a level of wealth which I'm proud to say is just as I had visualised it would be when I first started my own business.

Looking back, the first thing I had to do when approaching my own wealth-creation strategy was change my way of thinking. I had to go from thinking poor and cheap to thinking like the wealthy and the rich. This doesn't mean going out and buying Lamborghinis or Lear jets or eating in the best restaurants, but it does mean having a different approach to money, how you make it, how you use it, and how you keep it.

According to Donald Trump and Robert Kiyosaki's book *Why We Want You to be Rich*, the rich are getting richer and the poor are continuing to get poorer, and consequently the middle class will soon be nonexistent. The question you need to ask yourself is, where will you be? How you answer that question is the key to the psychology of money that I'm talking about. If you answered, 'I'll probably end up being poor,' then that's probably where you will end up. The first step is for you to believe, know and want to be rich. Most people these days play it safe and they do this because they are uncomfortable getting uncomfortable. They invest in safe investments, cling to job security and live below their means. In contrast, the people who are wealthy are those who are prepared to get uncomfortable in order to achieve their dream.

Our financial problems are caused by the way we think, and this is what we need to change. The scary thing is that people think that their pension and or superannuation or even the stock market will be enough to sustain them once they retire. But sadly, it won't. If we as individuals are not creating an asset base to carry us through retirement, especially when we're likely to be living longer, we can and will grow further into debt.

The good news is there's something you can do about it. It's never too late, no matter how old you are, to start building your asset base. I encourage you to get some financial education. You need to understand the difference between assets and liabilities. You need to know what passive income is and how it will become your road to easy street. The other piece of good news is that anybody can do it. Some of the most successful and wealthiest people in the world are less educated than you and I. What they do have however is financial savvy which comes mostly from common sense, but also from learning about the technology and psychology of money.

If you are always worried from week to week and month to month about just being able to pay the bills, then you're never going to get ahead financially.

I'm surprised at how many people don't even know their expenses versus their income. But one simple bit of common sense is if you are spending more than you are making, you're not creating wealth. Create a budget and know exactly how much you earn each month versus how much you spend.

Start to financially educate yourself, and the list of books at the back of this book is a great starting point. From *The Barefoot Investor* to *Rich Dad Poor Dad*, *The Art of the Deal* and *Secrets of the Millionaire Mind*, there are some terrific and interesting books out there written by experts that will help you on the way.

There are a multitude of good courses to do with real estate and the share market which I'd encourage you to seek out. But a word of warning - there are also a lot of dodgy ones. Only go with the courses that are certified by leading real estate bodies or the stock exchange, and look out for sharks because they could end up putting you in a world of trouble.

The future belongs to those who are currently building an asset base. Assets put money in your pocket. Shares, property, owning businesses, owning parts of businesses and the like are all a means for you to gain additional cash flow. Liabilities take money out of your pocket. The goal when creating wealth is to have your assets throwing off more money than your expenses. If the investments you have - the ones you don't need to actively work in - are throwing off more money than your cost of living, then you are already on the road to wealth creation. My advice is to do a budget, work out where you sit, look at your assets or what assets you would like to accumulate over a period of time, and start to get financially educated.

The rich have a vision for five, ten, fifteen years ahead, and the rich accumulate assets. The level of risk is entirely up to you, and risk assessment will be part of your strategy in accumulating assets. The rich buy assets that will continue to grow in value while putting money in their pockets.

No matter what level you begin at, you must make a start. To know how to do this seek out assistance from professionals and begin to read more about wealth creation. At the very least I would suggest you read and reread *Rich Dad Poor Dad*. I think Robert Kiyosaki's book is amongst the most straightforward, easy to read, and profoundly powerful advice that you could put your hands on. Once you've read it, put it down, take some notes, and then re-read it. This book could make a lot of difference to your wealth-creation strategies and really is a great starting point.

iT'S ALRiGHT FOR YOU

Some people who are reading this chapter right now will be saying, 'It's alright for you', 'I could never do that', 'It's different for me because . . .' If that's what you are saying to yourself right now, then that is the first ceiling you need to remove in order to have the right Mojo mindset. That sort of ceiling will automatically steal your Mojo. The rich don't say to themselves, 'I could never do that, I could never afford that, it could never happen to me.'

The rich say, 'How do I make this happen, in what ways could I afford this, what do I need to do today to start moving towards it?' Hopefully the other side of your mind is saying, 'Well what if this is true? What if

I gave it a chance?' That's the beginning of the Mojo mindset.

For most people, once you have done a budget and established exactly where you're at with income, expenses, assets and liabilities, you can start to put in place the appropriate steps towards creating your wealth strategy.

If you have credit card debt then that should be the first thing that's targeted. Banks, building societies and credit unions profit from the overwhelming amount of debt we carry. If you owe money to a financial institution, friends or family and that loan is not putting money into your pocket, then it's a liability and needs to vanish. The only debt that is good is debt that is being used to fund income-generating assets such as real estate, shares or the purchase of a business.

In the back of your mind I know many of you are thinking that it couldn't happen to you. Well, let me give you a real-life example. I was working with a young guy who wanted to get a wealth-creation strategy in place. We had worked through many areas of his Mojo, including his relationship, health, fitness and business, and had moved on to wealth. At this point, my client had zero assets. He lived in a very expensive house in Sydney but that of course was a liability and not generating any income for him or his wife. Fast forward one year later - he had amassed an asset base of $1 million, and it was costing him just over $500 a month to service the loan for the $1 million. How had he done it? Well first he bought property in regional areas of Australia that he was familiar with. Secondly all the property he purchased, he rented out, and hence it became good debt because someone else was paying it off for him.

Years down the track his properties have achieved capital growth and he has benefited from the fact that tenants have been paying off his loans. Needless to say whenever I see him in the street he's all smiles, and he's thankful that he began his wealth-building strategy by changing his Mojo mindset.

Your mind is your most valuable financial asset. When your finances are in place it brings a smile to your face and it's certainly a great way to bring Mojo into all areas of your being. It's amazing how when your finances are under control you suddenly have more energy at work and at play.

GRAB A BOOK

Aristotle said that 'all men by nature desire to know'. Modern philosophers have explored the many ways in which people sabotage this natural thirst for knowledge through rationalisation and self-deception. In his book *Love is the Killer App*, Tim Sanders said, 'Reading is a source of potency, so manage it like an asset.'

Become a walking encyclopedia of answers for anyone who has questions. Those who know me well know that I'm a pretty serious reader and I have to say it has become one of my greatest assets during the last few years. Each year I set myself a target number of books to read. The reason I do this is because it motivates me to read more, finish books, and then look for the next new and exciting book to open. For me it is one of the greatest feelings to walk into a bookshop, find a new book, open it, smell the fresh pages, and know there are some great nuggets of learning within the covers. I never rush through a book. I savour each page and enjoy the quiet reading time.

It always surprises me how little reading people do. It's such a great asset, so why are we not building on it? The differences between the person you are today and the person you will be tomorrow are the things you read, the things you see and the people you meet. The easiest way to build your knowledge bank is to read. You may not want to set yourself a goal of a number of books to read in a year - maybe that won't work for you - but you do need to find your own way of making time to read.

I always carry a book with me no matter where I go. As is the way in society today, I'm constantly left waiting in receptions for people while they continue on with their work. So rather than just sitting and waiting, I pull out my book and start reading. A key point here, and something you might want to take on board, is to never wait for anybody! I always use my time to continue learning and to entertain myself. I always make sure I read at least a chapter each night before I hit the sack. As Jim Rohn the famous life coach once said, 'Miss a meal but never miss your reading.' If you don't have a book right now that's feeding your imagination, experiences and knowledge, then get one. Make a point of opening a book every day. Build your asset now and get ahead of the pack. Become a continuous learner - read, listen, ponder, question, and be curious!

SPEECHES

My cycling partner told me a great story about a speech he had delivered at a mate's wedding. It was exciting to hear the history these two guys had and about the speech that he presented in front of the guests at this special occasion. Later that morning once we'd finished our ride and I arrived home, it made me think about speeches and how so few occasions arise where the people who mean the most to us get to tell us what we mean to them. When you think about it the only time people ever make speeches to tell you how they feel about you is at your wedding, or probably your 21st birthday party. Apart from that the opportunities are few and far between for somebody to take to their feet and talk about you, your accomplishments, the sort of person you are, and what you mean to them. Maybe there's one other occasion, but chances are you won't be around for that one, because it will be your eulogy. I guess the question is, what can we do to change it?

Well there are a couple of things you might consider. Why just have a great party for your 21st or your wedding? Celebrate birthdays and special occasions, and at those times, invite close friends or relatives to say a few words. They don't need to be big elaborate parties, but quite often we save our celebrations only for big occasions. Life is not getting easier and along the way we should take the time to celebrate our accomplishments. Sometimes when your friends do make a speech about you and your accomplishments, it makes you sit back and reflect on some of the things that have gone well and the great things that you've done. This can be a great kick-start for your Mojo!

When somebody compliments you, accept it graciously and appreciate it. Quite often when people receive a compliment and they simply brush it aside due to embarrassment or lack of self-belief. Take compliments on board as they are a wonderful boost for your Mojo.

You also need to recognise how important it is for you to pass on compliments to other people. Although this book is about stealing back your own Mojo, it's just as important for you to help other people steal back theirs. Nothing fires you up more than a compliment. It costs nothing and it is simple, but it's surprising how few people do it. When you compliment somebody you fire up their Mojo, but seeing their reaction and the feeling you get from helping somebody feel good about themselves sparks your own Mojo as well.

Don't leave it to special occasions to tell someone how important they are, how great they are, that they've done something wonderful or that there's something you admire about them. This is Mojo at work at its best. 'Be genuine in your approbation and lavish in your praise,' is what Dale Carnegie said in his book *How to Win Friends and Influence People*. The book was written in the 1930s, and it is still as appropriate today as it was back then. As long as you are sincere and you look the person in the eye when you give the compliment then you can't do it often enough.

i CAN'T WAiT

In the movie *Billy Madison*, starring Adam Sandler, there is a particular scene where one of the children at school says to Billy Madison, 'I can't wait until I go to high school.' Adam Sandler's character Billy grabs the pudgy kid by the cheeks and gently shakes his head, saying 'Don't ever say that, stay here.' That scene really got me thinking about those people who say 'I can't wait until my holidays' or 'I can't wait until . . .' My concern is that these people are actually so looking forward to the future that they are paying little or no attention to the present. There is nothing wrong with looking forward to an upcoming event, the important thing to remember is that you live in the present moment and that you should enjoy each moment rather than wishing them away. Please don't make the mistake of wishing away time thinking that there's better to come, because once this moment is gone, you'll never see it again. Don't miss out on the present.

You may have heard of Gestalt Therapy, which was invented by Dr Frederick (Fritz) S. Perls. He was also someone who didn't believe in missing out on the present. He is quoted as saying that if you have one foot in the past and one foot in the future you're pissing on the present, which may be somewhat crude but it is also very true of a great many people. Those who worry and obsess about what's happened in the past or who fantasise and fixate on the future only miss out on the present moment.

I truly believe that it is important to celebrate each day that we are on this earth. The Hawaiians are particularly good at this, perhaps because they are surrounded by nature and a large expanse of ocean and it has become more a part of their lives than those living in large cities in mainland communities.

One afternoon towards sunset I was walking on the beach in Maui without many people around. However, within ten minutes or so the beach became suddenly quite crowded, and before I knew it I was amongst quite a large number of people without knowing why. I realised that the beach was full of locals who were coming down to the beach to watch the sunset. As the sun disappeared for the day, applause broke out across the beach in celebration of the end of another great day. Maui is a very spiritual and relaxed place. Time really does seem to slow, things seem much simpler, and the world seems to synchronise the way it should. The people of Maui celebrate every minute, really living in the moment in a calm, relaxed and enjoyable state that surely must stimulate their Mojo. It's probably why they are seemingly so relaxed and always smiling. This experience certainly made me appreciate just how quickly a single day passes. As the sun gets closer to the horizon you can almost see it disappearing before your very eyes.

I couldn't help thinking that in most large cities the setting sun is of no consequence in our daily lives. We allow our time to slip by without making any effort to appreciate each passing moment. If you don't love your job then you should find a job you do love so that you can begin to appreciate every minute.

Back in Chapter 1, 'Mojo Mindset', I referred to Sahar Hashemi, co-creator of the very successful Coffee Republic brand. Prior to becoming an entrepreneur and starting Coffee Republic with her brother, Sahar was a solicitor, however over time she realised that the job did not suit her personality. She strongly believes that if what you're doing doesn't suit you, then you must find the job or activity that does. In this way you will love getting out of bed every morning and you will appreciate every minute as it passes.

I feel sorry for people who don't love their job, who go to work because they feel as though they have to, and wish their time away anticipating only the next weekend or holiday. If you don't currently appreciate how quickly time is going, take a holiday to Maui, sit on the beach in Lahaina, and applaud the sunset with the locals. It makes you appreciate just how precious time is and how quickly it passes us by.

DON'T SEND A TELEGRAPH

When speaking with audiences about holding them-selves to a higher standard, some people get the impres-sion that in order to be outstanding, you have to act overly confident, pretentious, and in some cases a little arrogant. That simply is not the intention. Raising the roof is about building an inward confidence and internal standard that you hold yourself to. It certainly is not about walking around beating your chest.

In the book *How Lance Does It* the author, Brad Kearns, outlines how Lance Armstrong has become the cyclist, the leader, the ambassador and the man that he is. Lance has an inner confidence and an inner belief about himself and his mission or purpose. He wastes little energy on issues, or small talk that is unnecessary or time wasting. As Lance puts it, if you're a boxer and you telegraph your punches, you'll end up with a bloody nose. In the same way, people who are all talk and no action generally end up coming unstuck.

In an interview with Michael Parkinson, the actor Russell Crowe said when he sets himself a goal, he internalises it and lets it set until it brews inside of him to become a burning need, 'I don't waste energy talking about it,' he said. Instead, he internalises it and lets it grow until he either attracts the necessary people, steps or actions, or he starts to move forward himself.

Lance Armstrong is the greatest cyclist of all time, and Russell Crowe is one of our great modern day actors. It is possible for us to learn from how they do things and apply it to our own world, without necessarily having to consider ourselves future cyclists or movie stars.

In your own mind, in your own heart, set the standards, set the limits and don't stand for mediocrity. Don't waste your time, energy or your breath on unnecessary bragging, chest beating or making outlandish claims. No-one else need know your goals or your motivation, but you.

When I was in Texas in the USA, the Texan ranch hands had a great saying for people who are all talk no action - in Texas they say they are big hat, no cattle.

KEEPING THE ROOF RAISED

One thing I've come to appreciate is that quite often we set lofty goals or dreams for ourselves and only celebrate at the very end. Through my running and cycling I have learned that it's important to set milestones along the way and celebrate those milestones as you achieve them. Generally when I was preparing myself for a marathon my visualisation, plans, and program were all set for that one day, four or five months away.

I learnt to celebrate milestones when I joined a new marathon training squad. At training sessions we would do repetitions of varying distances from 300 metres to one kilometre. I was surprised when some of the younger members of the squad, some of them a third of my age, would approach me after sessions, and ask 'How did you go tonight?' We would then talk about each training session, and each repetition, and how far away we were from our personal bests.

If, during the training session, you were able to achieve a personal best, or PB, there was such a great feeling of satisfaction - yet it was only a training session. What I learned from my much younger training partners is that you must enjoy the journey, and when you achieve milestones along the way, celebrate. It was something as simple as a pat on the back and a big grin that gave me the feeling of satisfaction, as I drove home from each training session, knowing that I'd cracked a PB, and yet knowing the marathon was still months away.

I brought this topic up in a presentation to a large radio group in Sydney some time ago. As I talked through the milestones, reward and celebration concept, the General Manager raised his hand to make a point in front of the group. He said the same thing was appropriate in his business, where he was overseeing the sales representatives in his sales team. He said if it got to the 24th or 25th of a given month, and the team had achieved budget, the very next statement was normally 'How are we looking for next month?' He said they never stopped to celebrate that they had achieved or even exceeded budget for the month they were in. It was always an automatic thought of 'Well that job's done, now what?' This probably contributes to a great deal of burn out in many industries, community and social groups, because we're always setting bigger and better goals, but very rarely do we stop along the way and celebrate our success.

Now when I say celebrate success, this can simply be, like my experience with my running squad, where it's a pat on the back and a big wide grin. It could also be rewarding yourself with a massage, a coffee with a friend, or a new book, if you achieved a certain goal in health, fitness, work, a social sense or a family environment. The size of the reward is entirely up to you.

What's most important is the fact that you step back, celebrate success and reward yourself before moving on to the next milestone. We are often very hard on ourselves in terms of setting goals and goal achievement. But along the way there's a lot to be said for stopping, taking a breath, dropping your shoulders and consciously rewarding or thanking yourself for achieving a milestone.

Something else to consider is celebrating the milestones of someone else who has set themself a task. Whether it's losing weight, getting fit, entering a sporting event, opening a new store, achieving a business goal, or getting a promotion, its important that we stop and celebrate these milestones with those around us. Simply buying somebody a cup of coffee as a celebration of an achievement is more than adequate. Its not the coffee, its not the shopping spree, it's the acknowledgement of a job well done.

For me there was nothing like the feeling of crossing the line after 42.2 kilometres, in a marathon and having achieved a goal, a personal best, or placing in a race. It was the ultimate sense of satisfaction to share the result with family, friends and comrades. But in hindsight, why wait till the end of the four month training period to celebrate, when we can do it every day of every week on the road to our bigger goals? Remember, treating, rewarding and celebrating is not about having to spend a lot of money, it's Mojo thinking, and it's a Mojo mindset.

MOJO CHECK-UP

✓ What are my ceilings right now?
✓ Am I holding myself to a standard of outstanding?
✓ Am I stuck in a mediocre rut?
✓ If I had no limits, what would I do?
✓ What is going well for me?
✓ Am I stretching?
✓ Do I need a break?
✓ Am I living or just existing?

CHAPTER 3
COUNCIL

People with Mojo not only attract but they actively look to surround themselves with the right people. This chapter is all about the importance of establishing your own council of advisers. It's about looking at the people you surround yourself with and making decisions about who you want to spend more time with; that is, those people who give you Mojo. It's also about how to engage with those people in meaningful conversations and how important it is to give as much to those people as you would hope to receive in return. Whether in person, on the telephone, in meetings or via electronic communication, there are very simple ways to build Mojo.

When I crossed the finishing line at the Boston Marathon in 2002 I achieved my goal of finishing in the top ten per cent of this elite field. However, being the type of person I am, I wasn't satisfied with that result and I wanted to set myself a more challenging goal. On my return to Sydney I decided to create a new council as I realised that to extend myself on the marathon front I would have to stop training with my current triathlon squad and find a running coach who knew marathons. I also decided to find a physiotherapist and a chiropractor who understood my body and who had worked with champions. Although I wasn't an elite athlete myself, I wanted to be surrounded by the very best people to help me achieve my goals.

I did my research, and within a year I had found a squad to train with who were amongst the best in the country, and I had also found my physiotherapist and chiropractor. I was also running marathons 15 minutes quicker than I'd ever run them before. How was this possible? Partly because of my Mojo mindset, partly because of my nutrition and care for my body, but also because I surrounded myself with the right council. I'd been a great believer in the importance of great council in the business arena for close to ten years, but before this time I had not thought to apply the philosophy to other areas of my life.

I have a council for my wealth creation, and have had the same bank manager, tax adviser, bookkeeper and lawyer for seven years. They know me, they know my philosophies, they work hard, and I reward them well for it. I also have councils in place for my family and personal life, business, support and learning. When I had to have surgery on the cartilage in my right knee, I even set about creating a council in preparation for the operation - I made sure my surgeon, physiotherapist, chiropractor and nutritionist all communicated with each other throughout the planning, operation, recovery and rehabilitation period in order to create the best possible outcome.

Now you may think that's a lot of council. You may prefer to have just one council who is your support team for everything you do in life. The important thing to realise is that you can't do it all on your own. You need to have the right people around you to support, encourage and celebrate with you through good and bad. Most people don't take the time to actually sit down and think about who they might like to have in their council.

If you've never thought about who your council might be then now is a good time to turn to the back of the book and make some notes. During the hard times, who are the people who walk in the door when everybody else is walking out? Who are the people who are genuinely happy to see you succeed? Who is first on the scene when things aren't going so well, to comfort, assist, aid and encourage?

You may find there are some gaps in your council of advisers, and perhaps this will create an opportunity for you. I've always found that once you have identified some gaps in your council or areas of your life that would benefit from having a council, it's amazing how people suddenly appear, either through contacts or new acquaintances, who could potentially become great members of your council.

You will find that your Mojo will increase just from knowing that you have the right people around you, people who have your best interests at heart. These are people you can turn to when your Mojo is down, and they can help you get back on track. Mahatma Gandhi said 'A friend is someone who knows the song in your heart and can sing it back to you when you have forgotten the words.' What a beautiful way to think of friendship.

In his book *What it Takes to Be #1* about the legendary American football coach Vince Lombardi, Vince Lombardi Jr said that his father firmly believed in creating the right team. He said his father always maintained that in order to have a committed team you had to get rid of those who were uncommitted. In some cases you may look at your council and realise you've surrounded yourself with a number of people who are in fact sucking the Mojo out of you, people who just don't share the same goals, dreams, desires or energy that you have. In this situation you may need to free them from your council, which is not to say that you can no longer associate with them, it's just that they may not be the right people to have closest to you. People in your council are the ones who are enthusiastic in their desire to see you succeed, and if you find you have less than committed people around you it may be time to make a few changes.

In her book *Black, White and Gold*, British athlete Dame Kelly Holmes discussed her achievements at the 2004 Olympic Games in Athens. For almost ten years Kelly had been dogged by injury. Then at the 2004 Games she won not only the women's 800 metre final but she doubled up to win the 1500 metre final. Overnight she became a British hero. Kelly believes that this turning point in her career came when she created a new council. She found a new coach, physiotherapist, nutritionist, a chiropractor, massage therapist, and she trained with world champion women's 800 metre athlete Maria Mutola. Kelly believes that creating the right council helped her have an injury-free lead-up to the Games and consequently two incredible victories in Athens.

Rock group U2 sum it up in their song, 'Sometimes you can't make it on your own.'

LISTEN UP

Sadly, the art of conversation is something that has been lost in our modern society. Most people who are engaged in conversation with others aren't even hearing what the other person is saying, they are simply waiting for their turn to talk. When you are engaged in a conversation, are you really listening? Yes, yes, of course you are . . . but are you *really*?

I was working out at the gym recently when I noticed a young guy making his way onto a treadmill. Once the machine was set to a slow walk and the platform started to move he immediately picked up his mobile phone and made a call. For twenty minutes he slowly walked on the machine while chatting on the phone. Was he really engaged in either of these activities? No! Not only was he wasting his precious time on the treadmill, he was also far from giving the person on the other end of the phone his full attention. Instead he was looking at the machine, glancing at the attractive girls around him, and watching the giant television screens in his immediate vicinity.

I then looked out the window at the block of units neighbouring the gym. A young lady was enjoying the sun with her telephone tucked under her arm and the receiver tucked under her ear. While she chatted to her friend, she weeded the garden, picked up some rubbish, rearranged the furniture, and did her toe nails. Oh, and of course she was totally engaged in the telephone conversation she was having . . . sure!

When you're engaged in a conversation either face to face or on the telephone, the most powerful thing you can do for the other person is to show them the decency of giving them your full attention.

When you are having a conversation just listen and just talk. Don't try to exercise, eat, read a magazine, do the housework, or even worse, speak when someone else is speaking. *Really* listening means being fully focused and fully engaged with the person with whom you are talking . . . their words, tone, body language (if you can see it), and feelings. This is hard to do when you're engaged in another activity or two. We have all sat at our desk in conversation on the phone, while we check emails, flick through a magazine or eat a snack.

Meanwhile we're not doing any of these things particularly well, and worse still, our minds are so busy we cannot think clearly about what is being said to us. We're also not reading effectively, eating properly, or thinking creatively.

There are conversations happening around us all the time in which people are simply exchanging statements. The art of conversation is really very simple, yet most people don't put the time into it. Be patient, be curious, be interested and be genuine. That's the secret of having Mojo in your conversations. Once people have enjoyed their conversation with you they will wonder what it is that makes speaking with you so different and so much better than speaking with others.

HOOKiNG

Earlier we looked at the skills involved in questioning and listening efficiently. Training programs, audio tapes, books, lectures and even television programs offer guidance to unlocking the secrets of effective listening. As I've said before, it is not that hard to be a good listener. Anybody can improve their listening skills with a little effort, but it's surprising how few people will put in that effort.

A great way to help improve your listening skills is to use what I call 'hooking'. This process is simple, and I have always received very positive feedback from those who have used it.

The US talk show host David Letterman hooks one question out of another. What do I mean by that? Well, whenever Letterman asks a question, he actually listens to the answer and uses a piece of that answer as a hook for the next question. Here's an example of what I mean:

David: 'So Jack, what have you been doing for the holidays?'

Jack: 'I went up to my holiday home in Colorado.'

David: 'What sorts of things do you do up in
Colorado?'
Jack: 'Mostly skiing and snowboarding.'
David: 'Are you a good snowboarder?'

And so it goes. David Letterman really listens to what is said by his guests, and simply finds something interesting in the answer to act as a hook for the next question. It is a simple and easy-to-use tool to enhance your listening skills. People love to talk, and especially love to talk about themselves. If you keep that in mind it will lead to very interesting conversations. You'll find that people enjoy speaking with you because they feel as though you are really listening.

So many people just talk *at* each other and never really give consideration to or show interest in what the other person has said. Often when someone else is talking we just sit there and wait for our turn to speak. Some people don't even wait for the other person to finish before they start to speak over the top of them, so imagine what an impact a simple thing like hooking can have. People will recognise you as a good listener, an interesting person to talk to, and who knows, even a potential talk show host! This simple process will certainly bring Mojo into your interactions with others, and people will appreciate the fact that you engage in real conversations.

The hooking process also makes it much easier to engage in conversations with complete strangers and alleviate any embarrassing or somewhat strained period of silence in a conversation. I've used hooking at parties, functions, in the workplace, and with clients. You simply ask one open-ended question, actually *listen* to the answer, and then hook the next question out of something within that answer. Believe it or not, Prince Charles employs a similar method. Whenever you hear Prince Charles speaking he asks a question, repeats a key response from the person he is speaking with, and from that he will ask the next question. Imagine the number of conversations that he would have every day with complete strangers. Yet people walk away believing he is a charming man, interesting in conversation, and someone that on some level has Mojo.

E-MOJO

Have you ever sat and pored over an email, reading it forwards and then backwards over and over again, all the while working yourself into a frenzy wondering what the writer's intention was? The meaning of an email is quite often misinterpreted by the reader either due to the wording or as a result of the tone of the email.

Here is a simple way to approach emails that will enable you to create Mojo electronically. When you want to compliment someone, do it in writing. When you want to address an issue or discuss something you're not happy about, do it verbally, or even better do it in person. Why?

When you send an email that has a negative slant to it the recipient can quite easily misinterpret its meaning.

Although it may have been meant one way it can easily be misconstrued and taken the wrong way, completely stealing Mojo away from you and the email itself. The recipient responds by addressing the tone that has been interpreted, and fires back a reply that is equally misconstrued, so what could have been a simple misunderstanding turns into a giant bushfire that takes up energy, time and focus, stealing Mojo from everyone involved.

In contrast, this tendency actually becomes a positive when the email is complimentary. When an email is complimentary we can read it over and over again and no matter how it's interpreted, it makes us feel great! So remember, if you want to praise someone, do it in writing. If someone has done something less than pleasing, or in your opinion, not well, then address it face to face or at least by telephone. Never chastise, dress down or address negative issues in writing.

There's no question you can have Mojo stolen in writing. You can also very easily steal someone else's Mojo in writing, so be very aware of this when you let your fingers do the talking. We live in an age where an increasing amount of communication is done via technology. Just be wary about having your Mojo stolen by email, or worse still, stealing somebody else's. Also remember that it is possible to help someone steal their Mojo back simply by being aware of the way you write to them.

MOJO CHECK-UP

✓ Do I need to make changes to my council?
✓ Have I checked in with my council?
✓ Should I catch up with my council?
✓ Should I thank my council?
✓ Do I need a new perspective?

CHAPTER 4
FAT BASTARDS

I've taken the title for this chapter from the Mike Myers film *Austin Powers 2 - The Spy Who Shagged Me*. Fat Bastard was the larger than life character who stole Austin Powers's Mojo, so I use 'fat bastards' to describe people who can steal your Mojo as well as the fat bastards in our own minds; that is, the thoughts that create doubt and steal away our Mojo.

LITTLE VOICES

One of the greatest challenges or ceilings we all face, no matter what age we are, is controlling the little voice inside our head. Henry Ford once said, 'If you think you can or you think you can't, either way you're right.' The little voice inside your head can cause enormous havoc with your Mojo. But the little voice is your *own* voice and you can control it. How much control you have over that voice is entirely in your hands.

To explain, I will use the analogy of golfers walking up to the golf tee. They walk up to the green, tee up the ball, and at the back of their mind, they're saying, 'Don't hit it in the water, don't hit it in the water' . . . and you can guarantee where the ball is going. These golfers are concentrating on where they *don't* want the ball to go instead of where they *do* want the ball to go. That little voice is essentially programming them to put the ball into the water.

Remember, the brain doesn't know the difference between what is real and what is imaginary, and when you program that little voice inside your mind you're essentially programming yourself for either success or failure. Now, that little voice will always be saying that there's something you can or can't do, but the important thing is to make sure there's a louder voice inside your mind saying 'Yes I can'. With practice you will learn to put aside the negative voice and make the voice of positive reinforcement louder.

What you need to do when that little voice begins to create doubt, concern, low self-esteem or negativity in your mind is practise saying to yourself, 'No, I can do this.' A lot of the time there's no basis for the negative talk and no basis for the belief that something cannot work. It comes back to that feeling of being uncomfortable, and when we don't understand something we tend to make assumptions. In most cases we assume that we have limits or ceilings over ourselves, so the little voice succeeds in talking us out of things. On the occasions where the voice does rear its ugly head, it's important that you assure yourself there is no rational basis for the negativity and start to view things from a more positive perspective. You need to be able to say to yourself, 'I can do this, I'm capable of doing this and I'm going to give it my best shot.' The more you do it and the more you take control of that voice, the easier you'll find it.

This is the point where your Mojo mindset plays its part. At any given moment when you hear that little voice inside your head, you need to remind yourself that you have two choices; to listen to that little negative voice, or to listen to the roar of positivity and power coming from the other side. It really is a choice. Any successful person - whether their success is a sporting achievement, business or social endeavour, politics or community effort - will tell you that they had doubts about whether they would succeed. However, over time they have learnt to control their doubts by using their Mojo mindset. Remember the past does not equal the present - just because something happened in the past does not mean it has to happen again.

I was watching an interview recently with Raelene Boyle, one of Australia's greatest athletes who won numerous gold medals for Australia and then faced even greater challenges when she endured not one but two bouts of cancer. In the interview Raelene made the point that outstanding people have the ability to bounce back time and time again. In their minds they know that just because something happened in the past doesn't mean that it is going to repeat itself in the future. These people find the power to put aside the voice of doubt or the fat bastard, and replace it with a loud proud voice.

WHO STOLE MY MOJO?

THE OTHER FAT BASTARDS

The other voices we need to be very aware of in our own minds are the voices of other people. There's no question that other people's opinions can also create an environment that steals our Mojo away from us.

At times I have been guilty of allowing other people's ideas to influence my thinking, and in turn to drag down my self-esteem. When I worked in the corporate world I let the opinions or actions of others cause me to lose confidence, momentum, and certainly take away from my Mojo. When you focus too much on what other people say, it can be very damaging to your ego and self-esteem, and this can have a dramatic effect on your career and personal life. Relationships often break down in these circumstances as we spend so much time dwelling on work and worrying about the politics of the business that we end up taking it home with us in the evening.

Marcia Hines is one of Australia's greatest entertainers and, after more than three decades, is still at her best. When Marcia was interviewed by Andrew Denton on the ABC's *Enough Rope*, he asked Marcia about her daughter Deni, who is a very successful recording artist in her own right. He asked Marcia whether she ever felt threatened by the beauty and talent of her daughter. Marcia looked Andrew in the eye and said bluntly, 'I don't compete with anybody; the only person I compete with is myself.' And this is why Marcia has been so successful in the demanding and often unforgiving entertainment industry. What a brilliant attitude. This comment sent me running for my journal, as I felt it summed up so much of what I had been through in my own career. Quite often I have found myself so concerned with the opinions of others, competing with them on their level, that I've forgotten to actually hold myself to my own standards. Raising the roof, as you saw in the previous chapter, is all about holding yourself to a higher standard. It's not about comparing or competing, it's about you and your standards - the rest will take care of itself.

Karl Lagerfeld is regarded as a fashion genius and a leader in the world of fashion. He has been the designer behind fashion houses such as Chanel and Fendi, and now has his own very successful brand in Lagerfeld. I saw Karl Lagerfeld interviewed on a television show when he was asked to judge the winner of a fashion photography competition. A talented photographer himself, Karl Lagerfield said, 'I find it very hard to do this. I only know how I am, not how others are. I never compare, I never compete. That's how I live my life.'

If we were all to take a leaf out of Karl Lagerfeld's book, we would find it much easier to take back our Mojo and protect our minds from fat bastards. Instead of competing with our neighbours, the person in the cubicle next to us, or the person across the hall, we should adopt a 'never compete never compare' attitude, and refocus our energy onto ourselves and what we can do in order to raise the roof in our own lives and build our Mojo. No doubt this is also why Karl Lagerfeld has been such a driving force in the world of fashion for so many years. He doesn't follow other trends, other designers, or other styles. Instead he leads and creates his own voice.

In business, in sport, in friendship, and in spirit, it's about knowing what you want and how you are going to get there, and not competing or comparing yourself to others. Let go of the voices of the fat bastards that surround you and know that as long as you have your own goals, your own visions and your own plans, and if you're honest and disciplined in your approach, then good things will happen. Maybe Mark Twain said it best when he said, 'Keep away from people who try to belittle your ambitions. Small people always do that, but the really great ones make you feel that you too can become great.'

MY PERFECT RACE

I had the opportunity to have a coffee with British Olympian Roger Black after we had both presented at a conference. A 5-time European champion, Commonwealth Games gold medallist and Olympic silver medallist in Atlanta in 1996. He is well known in Britain for his incredible achievements on the track as well as for his subsequent successful media and speaking career. Roger and I discussed one of the questions asked during the presentation he had just given. The audience member asked Roger if when he lined up in the blocks on the starting line in Atlanta in the 400 metres against the eventual winner Michael Johnson, in his own mind he really believed he could beat him.

Roger said he had often pondered that question and was being honest when he replied that the answer was no.

In his mind he never thought he could beat Michael Johnson. In fact he went on to explain that he never even gave a thought to beating Michael Johnson when he lined up on the blocks that day. Instead Roger concentrated and focused on one thing, and that was running his perfect race. Roger had spent his life endeavouring to run his perfect race, and on that day in Atlanta in 1996 he believes he ran it. In fact, he thinks of his Olympic silver medal as his gold medal.

Roger Black is a great example of how focus can alter your attitude to winning and the results you achieve. Everybody has the power of focus within them, the problem is that most people focus on all the things that might go wrong, as opposed to focusing on what they do want to happen. I agree with Donald Trump when he says, 'As long as you're going to be thinking any way, you may as well think big.'

Each day when you approach a meeting, approach your goals, go to the gym, or look to be the best mum or dad you can be, think about your focus. Do you focus on all the things you don't want to happen, or do you focus on all the things you do want to happen, and visualise the outstanding achievements you would like to see in your day, your week and your life? There's an old saying, 'Be careful what you focus on, you might just get it.'

SEND ME BACK TO MCDONALD'S

I've always been a great fan of the rock artist Pink. I think she is a wonderful performer and her attitude and confidence are to be admired. I remember hearing Pink interviewed about the success of her first album. When released it immediately garnered the attention of all the large record companies and she was swamped with recording offers. She finally signed with a record company for a second album, but no sooner had she signed than they asked her to make a large number of changes to the planned album. They wanted it produced differently - different cover, different style of music, different style of song writing, and they were in effect forcing their own ideas and image of Pink upon her. So Pink said point blank to the producers, 'I'm not doing it, send me back to McDonald's.'

During the interview Pink said that by that time in her career, she had enough confidence in her own ability to stand up for herself and not give in to other people's opinions about her music. She was going to do it her way or she wouldn't do it at all. If she couldn't record and perform her own music the way that she wanted, she would rather go back and work at McDonald's. Pink said you have to have the courage to back yourself. She also said that she would have burned out if she didn't have an opportunity to take risks.

Sometimes in order to stretch yourself you have to back yourself and go against the odds. Many great performers, businesspeople, community leaders and social leaders have had to buck the system in order to achieve greatness. Keep Pink's attitude in the back of your mind - you may lose a few challenges along the way but the ones you do win will bring joy, confidence, self-esteem and Mojo.

PRiMARY QUESTiONS

I attended a conference some time back where the presenter, Anthony Robbin, taught us a new technique called Primary Questions. He said that people's language programs their minds to achieve specific outcomes. As I mentioned earlier, the brain doesn't know the difference between what's real and what's imaginary, and when that little voice inside your head starts firing off comments, your brain then searches for evidence to back them up. In fact, what that means is that your brain starts to make it happen. It's the same thing when people are faced with a situation or problem and they start to program themselves with questions like, 'Why does this always happen to me?', 'How come I'm always in this situation?', 'Why am I so depressed?' or 'Why is the world so tough on me?' Essentially what is happening is that these questions are programming your outcomes, and while we continue to think in terms of questions such as these, we're really programming our thinking and consequently our actions to occur along these lines.

It is possible however to take control of a lot of the outcomes in our world by changing the primary questions we ask ourselves. In the book *Rich Dad Poor Dad*, Robert T. Kiyosaki said that his poor dad would always say, 'I can't afford something,' whereas a rich dad would always say, 'How can I make enough money to buy that?' It all comes down to the way you frame the questions.

My primary question is always 'What else?' By programming myself to ask 'What else?', I am forever looking at new and different options as to how things could be done. 'What else?' leads me into 'What's another way, how could I do it differently, what could I change, what could I add and what could I take away?' and so on. 'What else?' creates options, and when you are creating options you are using your creative mind.

I am never satisfied with only one way of doing something, especially if it's the way that everyone has always done it or it's the way society says it should be done. I'm normally the square peg in the round hole, and consequently 'What else?' is a very empowering question for me. Consider what *your* primary question might be, so when faced with negative or seemingly disempowering statements, you can simply recall your primary question and begin to uncover new possibilities and new ways of approaching things.

This is an incredibly powerful tool for helping you take control of the fat bastards in your mind, and you will find that the outcomes can be very positive. One lady I work with always has a primary question of 'How can I make this great?' Whether she is talking about her family, her work, her sport or her hobbies, this woman is always trying to make things great and not just good. Terrific primary question. Maybe inadvertently you already have your primary question sorted, and if that is the case that's great, but if you haven't, then take some time to think today or over the next couple of days about what your primary question might be. It is a great way of reframing and creating the right Mojo mindset.

Being a cowboy at heart, I watched a reality show, called *Beyond the Bull*, about the 2006 World Championship Professional Bull Riding series in Las Vegas. I find that bull riding and life have a lot of parallels, and this is probably one of the reasons that I'm so drawn to the sport. The Las Vegas PBR event is the last one in the PBR series and attracts the world's best bull riders, all competing for one million dollars and the title of World Champion.

In the finals, two-time world champion bull rider Adriano Moralis was about to lower himself onto the back of a bull that weighed just over one tonne and said, 'I believe I can ride any bull in the world, the only enemy is my own mind.' That's why Adriano Moralis is a two-time world champion and may one day soon be the first person to add a third title to his record. What a terrific attitude!

Midway through the PBR event bull rider J.W. Hart, was speaking about the previous night's event where he had been bucked off in 3.6 seconds - a very disappointing result. As he mounted the chutes for his next bull ride that day he said, 'I got bucked off last night, but at 12.01 this morning it was another day and time to cowboy up.' This is the cowboy spirit that attracts me so much to the sport. Sure, you're going to go through some hard times and sure the fat bastards both in and out of your head are going to be trying to steal your Mojo away, but just like J.W. Hart says, at 12.01 each day it's another day, and the past does not equal the future. Don't let the fat bastards get you down, learn from the past and know that every day is another opportunity for you to steal back your Mojo.

MOJO CHECK-UP

✓ What is my primary question?
✓ Am I focusing on what I *do* want or what I *don't* want?
✓ Am I letting others get into my thoughts?
✓ Am I worried about what others think?
✓ Am I aware of the fat bastards in my own mind?
✓ What voice do I need to quieten? What does the other voice say?

CHAPTER 5

FEELiNG GROOVY BABY

Have you ever wondered why some people seem to have an extra bounce in their step, a twinkle in their eye, and a general sense of vitality about them? Or why some people have the extra clarity of thought and talent to be organised so that they can sort through the jumble and find an appropriate way forward?

This chapter is all about how to put more energy and vitality into your day and boost your Mojo. I don't mean that in just an energy sense, but also through clarity of thought and activity.

THE 70 PER CENT RULE

Before we go any further, on one of the blank pages at the end of this book, I'd like you to write down everything you drank and ate yesterday. From drinks - soft drinks, water, coffee, tea - to snacks, breakfast, lunch, dinner, treats . . . the whole lot. This is not a test, and no-one else has to see your list, but take the time to do it as it will help you get the most out of this part of the book. If you really don't want to write it down, then at least take the time to think through what you ate yesterday. Yes, I know, I know . . . yesterday wasn't a good day, and it was the exception to the rule - I'd love a dollar for every time I've heard that from an audience member!

Now answer me this - what percentage of the body do you think is made up of water? If you said 70 per cent, you would be right! My belief is that in order to maximise your energy, efficiency and productivity, you need to ensure that 70 per cent of what you put into your body is water-based or 'live' food. What do I mean by that? Essentially live food is food that you consume in the same form that nature produced it. Or, another way to explain it is if you were to put it in the ground, it would literally grow.

Given that such a large proportion of the body is water, the more natural water-based foods you put into it, the more effectively it will operate. The human body is an incredible organism, and for it to operate at its peak it needs the right fuel. Without the right fuel, the human body cannot produce the energy demanded on a daily basis, and consequently your Mojo levels drop away.

There are many great books that explain the science behind this concept, however for the purposes of this book the simple message is that if you want to regain your Mojo, you need to eat live foods. Hippocrates said 'Let food be thy medicine.' By eating naturally you'll increase your energy, your vitality, your sex drive and your immune system. And that being the case, it will be much easier for you to fight off colds, flu and other illnesses. And a more efficient digestive system will mean that you'll be less likely to experience organ malfunctions over time.

To ensure that your diet is 70 per cent live food, you need to include some fruit, vegetables, nuts, seeds, legumes and whole grains at each meal. Instead of just snacking on biscuits for morning and afternoon tea, or indulging in unhealthy treats throughout the day, try having a piece of fruit, a handful of nuts, some seeds, or chopped up vegetables with dip instead. It's actually not as hard as it sounds to eat well. The hardest part is changing to a Mojo mindset of eating for energy, eating for vitality and eating for Mojo, as opposed to just eating things because they taste good.

By ensuring that your diet is 70 per cent live food you'll also be getting rid of the excessive processed food from your diet. Processed foods are just that - foods that have been processed to within an inch of their life, and have little or no nutritional value or energy associated with them at all. The problem with processed food is that if you don't have an active lifestyle and the energy is not burned off, then the energy will eventually turn to fat. By changing your outlook and eating for vitality your body will naturally start to shed any excess fat.

You don't have to give up your treats completely. If you make sure your diet is predominantly live foods, then you can afford to have your treats. The problem is that most people have a live food intake of 30 per cent or less. Quite often in my speeches the majority of audience members will realise their intake of live food is less than ten per cent. They wonder why they always feel sluggish, tired, have no energy, have no sex drive and always feel bloated. Little wonder, when their diet is predominantly processed food that is stealing their Mojo.

SAY NO TO WHITE

During an episode of her television show, Oprah Winfrey said that one of the ways she was able to control her weight and stay healthy was to say 'no to white'. Naturally the studio audience broke out into raucous laughter, but after everyone had settled down, Oprah explained that by saying no to white, you avoid sugar and other highly processed foods such as flour and dairy. Now I acknowledge that Oprah's dietary habits are often short-lived, but I happen to believe that what she said had considerable merit. Foods that are highly processed have had pretty much all their nutritional value sucked out of them. Sugar, flour, fats and dairy add little to our health but steal energy and Mojo from our day, week and life.

If you want to reclaim your Mojo you must cut back dramatically on sugar. Fat is not the enemy anymore. The new enemy is sugar. It's hidden in all the processed food you buy from the corner store or the supermarket. If you read food labels carefully you'll see that most packaged products - that is, those that aren't natural - are very high in sugar. Sugar that is not burned off through exercise or a busy lifestyle, will turn into fat for both males and females. One of the biggest health issues facing our society right now is the massive amount of sugar that is being consumed through breakfast cereals, cookies, lunches, burgers, fries, pastas, cakes and so on. If you significantly reduce the amount of sugar, dairy, white wheat flour and pasta in your diet you'll see that you suddenly have so much more energy, and you'll feel the Mojo start to return to your life.

Now I don't believe in diets, as diets don't last. I do however believe in changing and maintaining healthy eating habits. The psychology of good health is about changing how you eat and doing it forever, not just for two or four weeks. Saying no to white is easy to remember, easy to understand, but for some people, very challenging. Changing your eating habits will take time, but once you feel the energy and Mojo start to return to your life, it will definitely make the changes much easier to maintain.

From a physical point of view, there are two activities that steal the most energy from you. The first is sex, and the other is digestion. I'm not going to focus on the sex side of things here, but if you get your Mojo back that part will take care of itself. Looking at the digestion side of things, if you think about how much is involved in digesting all the fat products, dairy goods and highly processed white goods you are eating, it's not hard to see where a lot of your energy is used. Your digestive system is taking so long to actually digest the food that it is not allowing you to draw energy from the food.

As I quoted earlier from Hippocrates, 'Let food be thy medicine.' Saying no to white is definitely one way to start allowing your food to be your medicine. By cutting out processed foods, and increasing your intake of live food you will very quickly start to feel and look 100 per cent better, and I guarantee you will have less illness in your life, all of which will build Mojo for you.

It is estimated that by 2050, 60 per cent of men and 50 per cent of women will be severely overweight. Currently in America 67 per cent of the population are overweight and 27 per cent are obese. A fatal heart attack happens every 4.5 seconds and 50 per cent of American males are likely to die of heart disease. These figures are astounding! Doctors, the science industry and the food industry are attributing a great deal of this situation to what we put in our mouths. In a recent edition of an Australian magazine called *Men's Health*, it was stated that in order for a male to have a six-pack stomach, 90 per cent of the effort had to be focused around diet. You can do as many sit-ups as you like but if your diet is nutritionally poor, you are wasting your time. Around a million drugs were prescribed in 2006 in the UK for obesity treatment. By 2025, the NHS costs of obesity is expected to rise to £5.3 billion. Our diet is literally killing us - not to mention that we're losing energy, we don't have the drive to get things done, and we're certainly, as a society, losing our Mojo.

I'M FULL

How often do you hear people finishing a meal and saying, 'I'm full'? Now I am a person who loves

FEELING GROOVY BABY

food, and if somebody puts Thai food or a nice buffet or roast in front of me, I am tempted to go back for seconds ... and probably thirds. However, this is not the way to eat for Mojo. In order to maximise the energy and efficiency of our systems we need to eat not only the right foods, but also the right amount. I'm the first to admit there are times when I over-eat. Consequently, I pay for it by feeling full and lethargic. Now, there are times when this is okay, such as at Christmas or on other special occasions, or on a Saturday night when you know the next day you are not going to require a great deal of energy and you are prepared to just kick back and relax. But on the whole, particularly during the week, we need to be more careful about how much we eat. If you want to steal back your Mojo and have the energy, desire, passion and clarity to get things done, then *don't* over-eat.

The right amount of food to eat is the amount that makes you feel comfortably full, as opposed to completely full. Many of us eat food because it's there in front of us, as opposed to only eating the food that will satisfy our hunger and fuel our energy requirements. Recently though, I've been experimenting with gauging the right amount of food. I now put less food on my plate and eat more slowly, and when I feel as though I'm reasonably satisfied, I stop eating. Many of us have been brought up to finish everything on our plate because there are less fortunate people than us going hungry. I can understand where this came from and I agree with the sentiment, but many of us probably have too much food on our plate to begin with. You should eat only what you need in order to satisfy your hunger and feel comfortably full.

As a guide, each meal should roughly consist of two handfuls of fruit and vegetables, one handful of good low-GI carbohydrates, and one handful of protein. Don't eat just for the sake of eating, because when you over-eat your digestive system does a lot more work to break down the food, and this requires a lot more energy. Consequently it leaves you with less energy to do other things you may want to do.

To get the most out of life and to get the most Mojo in your day, you need to have an efficient digestive system that's producing energy rather than wasting it. If you want your Mojo back, eat less food and eat better food, and see how great you feel.

iT'S ALL ABOUT HEART

It often amazes me how much time people waste exercising. This may seem like a strange thing to say given that exercise is an essential part of a healthy lifestyle, but when I say waste, I mean that there are people investing their valuable time going through the motions, but they aren't doing their exercise properly and therefore are not getting the best return.

Life is all about endurance. To build endurance we need to exercise in our ideal heart rate zone. You can calculate your maximum heart rate by deducting your age from 220. You should be exercising at a rate in between 65 per cent and 75 per cent of your maximum heart rate. In order to build endurance and steal back your Mojo, you need to keep your heart rate in between these amounts for a set amount of time when exercising. The other advantage is that you're teaching your body to burn fat and not sugar, and by burning fat you can go longer and harder at any activity you put your mind to.

You might ask, 'How do I know my heart rate?' There are a couple of ways to find out. You could buy a heart rate monitor; although it will cost you, it is the most accurate way of working out your heart rate. The heart rate monitor will also determine your optimum numbers for you, and be able to tell you step by step, stroke by stroke or pedal by pedal how successfully you are travelling towards your goals.

The other way to find your heart rate is to stop every so often and count your pulse for a ten-second period, then multiply that number by six. If you are exercising in a gym, most of the machines can tell you your heart rate. Most machines also allow you to pre-set your rates, and will automatically tell you whether you are above or below your optimum rate.

Another option is to make sure you are uncomfortable holding a conversation while you are exercising. If you are walking along and you can talk quite easily, then you're not walking quickly enough. Likewise if you're going along and you are finding it really hard to keep the conversation going without a lot of huff and puff, then you're probably going too hard. This is the secret to making exercise work for you in order to lose weight, feel great, steal back your Mojo and build your endurance for life.

For good health you should endeavour to spend thirty-five to forty minutes exercising at your ideal heart rate zone at least three times a week. You don't have to run until it hurts in order to get value for your exercise time. Go slower for longer and make sure you do it consistently and you will definitely be setting yourself up for good health.

There is an excellent book on all of this called *Slow Burn* by Stu Mittleman and Katherine Callan. Their philosophy is that you can achieve more by going slower, and focusing on how productive you can be while exercising. So find your heart rate zone and have the discipline to stick to it. As you can see it is something I feel passionate about, and it might sound a little challenging to start with, but once you work out the numbers and get started, you'll find it is quite a simple philosophy to follow. You can exercise by walking, running, working out in the gym, cycling, swimming or rock climbing. How you do it is irrelevant, just make sure that you do.

SLEEP ON IT

The body is very resilient and can do remarkable things when it has to. It is possible to be very productive on less than eight or nine hours sleep when necessary, but I also believe at some point your system needs to be replenished and it needs to rest. Our bodies are like a car; you can push them only so far before you need to put them in for a good service, tune up, change of oil, and a full tank of petrol.

I do not believe that you can live on three or four hours sleep each night, but I do realise that each individual requires their own optimum amount of rest for peak performance. I think sleep is a bit like a bank account. You can run it dry during the week, but every week or two you may need to have an afternoon sleep to replenish the account.

In the book *The 10 Rules of Sam Walton* by Michael Bergdahl that I referred to earlier, Bergdahl recalls working for the remarkable Sam Walton during the growth era of the world's biggest retailer, Walmart. Most staff arrived at 7 a.m. but Mr Sam, as he was known, used to arrive at work at 4 a.m. each morning. He believed that gave him the edge over his competitors because in those quiet moments he achieved more in that amount of time than in most of the other hours of the day. He believed that from 7 a.m. on, he was too busy in meetings and visiting his stores to really do any quality thinking. Sam Walton had a dream of what he wanted to achieve - the best retail chain in the world. Sam Walton's approach gave him the edge on his competitors and allowed him enough time throughout the day to manage his stores. It gave him the opportunity to walk around the stores and catch people doing great things, without having to worry about his emails, memos, planning and strategy.

Since I took up road cycling, I have been getting out of bed at 4.30 a.m. When I first started doing this I'll admit it was a shock to the system but now I wouldn't be without it. Three or four mornings a week I meet my riding buddies at 5 a.m. and we normally cycle for a couple of hours. Not only is it great camaraderie, but the feeling of having my exercise done by 7.30 in the morning is such a kick-start to my Mojo - I would not like to lose that feeling. But it's a mindset. As some of you read this and think 'insanity', others of you are saying 'what a great idea'. It's all to do with Mojo mindset. I agree with Sam Walton that this is a great way to get a jump on the world, and also once you've done it for a little while it just becomes part of your being.

Granted, I normally hit the sack at night at between 9.30 and 10 p.m., and on the weekend I normally have an afternoon snooze. But if you are having trouble fitting everything into your day, try getting up a half hour earlier in the morning. Does it really make a difference to your sleeping patterns? Not really, but it does give you an extra half an hour for reading, exercise, hobbies or just contemplating.

As I mentioned earlier, a lot of people lose sleep obsessing about their work, and one of the reasons they're doing so is because they haven't created enough interests in their life outside of work. Perhaps you are one of those people who lack creative endeavours away from the office. Unfortunately a lot of people determine their identity through their work, and because of this they do not put energy or time into other aspects of their life. One easy solution is to think about some other creative activity that you could do to take up some of the time that up until now has been spent at work or thinking about work. Perhaps you are interested in sculpting, writing, drawing, playing golf, scrapbooking, gardening, or some other pursuit that will not only distract you from your work but also stimulate your Mojo.

If it has been a while since you spent time on an activity outside of work and you aren't really sure what might interest you, then think about some of the things that you used to do when you were younger that caused you to completely lose track of time. What are some of the things that you may have done in the past, perhaps when you were a child, that were so exciting and absorbing they made you not give a second thought to food, or feeling tired? These are perhaps a good indicator of the types of activities that you have the greatest passion for. If you are unsure, ring your mum or dad, or go through old photo albums from when you were four, five or maybe even ten years old and think about the things that used to totally absorb you. When was the last time you did them?

I was recently in a session with a group who were considering this question, and a number of people told me they used to do gymnastics, play piano or work on their car. It was a great wake-up call for them, and as a result they created action plans in order to reintroduce themselves to the things they used to love doing. I received emails a few months later, telling me of the gains they've made in guitar playing or mountain bike riding, things they hadn't done since they were a kid.

After delivering a speech in London recently, I was approached backstage by a guy from the northern area of Britain. He had seen me speak the year prior and came up to share his story with me. He said that following on from the speech, he had realised that his passion was sailing. Since that time, he had bought a house closer to the water and his sailing was going so well that he was planning to try out in order to represent his country! As he told the story, you could see the excitement and adventure in his eyes, and he said he had certainly found the ticket to his Mojo.

Another thing you could try is to write down all the things that are on your mind regarding your work before you go to sleep. Rather than take them to bed with you, make a list of all the things you're thinking about and all the things that you have to do the next day. Once it's all written down, captured and sorted, you can let it go. If these thoughts come into your mind when you're about to fall asleep, just say to yourself gently, 'I've got that recorded, I've got it organised, I've got it sorted, I'll think about it tomorrow.'

Consider this lesson. A man walked up to a Zen master and said, 'Zen master, please teach me the secrets of Zen.' The Zen master replied, 'When working just work, when eating just eat, when resting just rest.' The man then replied to the Zen master, 'It can't be that easy.' The Zen master said, 'It is that easy yet it's amazing how few people can do it.'

The moral of the story is that when you're sleeping just sleep, and let everything else go. It is surprising how this simple tool can alleviate the troubles and worries from your mind. The only thing that causes you to lose sleep over your work is the thoughts in your own mind, and that is something that you have total control over. Try these simple tools. They work, and I've had great success in sessions with people from all over the world with them. Now that's something to sleep on!

DON'T BE ON TIME, BE EARLY

For years I worked in the corporate arena, and in that time I would have attended literally thousands of meetings. Looking back I would say that I was late for the majority of those meetings or, best-case scenario, I was lucky to arrive on time. I thought I had that uncanny ability of being able to time my journey to a meeting to the second. Whether on the other side of town, in another state, or just in the office next to mine, I would always leave at the very last minute. However, situations beyond my control regularly made me late. Even if by chance I was on time, I'd almost always arrive in a sweaty, flustered and annoyed state, exuding anything but Mojo.

Some years ago now I read an interesting book called *Slowing Down to the Speed of Life* by Richard Carlson and Joseph Bailey. That book changed my approach to time management completely. Carlson and Bailey discussed the concept of time and how to get the most out of yours. Central to their book was the premise that in order to get more out of your day you needed to slow down, which I found fascinating. Nowadays, rather than timing my departure to the last minute, I always build an extra ten or fifteen minutes into my travel time to allow for the 'stuff' that invariably happens.

Consequently I nearly always arrive at my meetings early, which gives me a chance to sit outside the venue or in the reception area before my speech or appointment, and take some time to go through what I'm about to speak about, read my notes, do some writing, or just sit and ponder. When I go into my meetings now, I feel as though my Mojo is far more evident as I've had a chance to collect my thoughts, visualise the meeting, and work out what I need to say. If you arrive at a meeting flustered, late and not in control, it is impossible to have your Mojo working at its peak capacity.

Time is one of our most precious commodities and it must be treated with respect. You can't manage time but you can manage how you spend your time. Consequently, rather than leaving it till the last minute and rushing to appointments, remember to build in some extra time which will enable you to arrive cool, calm and with your Mojo working. As formula one hero Jackie Stewart once said, 'Sometimes to be faster, we have to be slower.' So build in some time in your day and have it work to your advantage.

REMEMBER TO LOOK UP

To steal back your Mojo not only do you need to have a healthy body, you also need a healthy mind. Wherever you may be right now, I would suggest to you that you should just take a moment and literally 'look up'. Quite often as I head to and from meetings around the major cities of the world, I'm dodging crowds of people heading off to their corporate jobs for the day. It surprises me how difficult it is to make eye contact with any of these corporate robots. So often these people have their heads bowed, paying homage to their mobile phones, Blackberries or PDAs without a single thought as to what is going on around them.

I have been a pretty serious runner for a number of years, and I normally set off for a long run in the wee hours of Sunday morning. One morning as I headed down the main arterial road from the city towards Sydney Harbour with only street sweepers and the occasional bus for company, I looked up and saw the magnificent skyline of Sydney above me. It made me realise how little time we spend looking up, as opposed to ploughing headfirst into our daily lives focused on the steps immediately in front of us, or the mobile communication technology at our ear. At the airport, in the street or at the office, people are rushing along and not taking time to ponder issues or even what lies immediately ahead of them.

When you remember to look up, a number of things happen. The first thing is that you generally discover something of value or considerable beauty. Most people couldn't tell you what the ceiling of their office looks like, let alone the city skyline, their back yard, or the roof of their house. Secondly, you will probably find that by taking the time to look up, you relax. By looking up and taking a break to enjoy the skyline, trees, clouds or even a plane flying overhead, you can't help but relax and drop your shoulders.

It's also interesting that when people visualise and draw pictures in their mind, quite often they look up. If you ask a visual person a question, for example, 'What did you do on the weekend?', quite often you'll notice they tilt their head up slightly either to the left or right, or they look up with their eyes. Visual people are looking up to try to picture the answer in their mind. Although it sounds very simple, taking a moment to look up will not only provide a great forum for visualising the issue, problem or concern you have, but it also allows you time to ponder.

If nothing else, looking up gives you a good chance to take a moment to relax, centre your thoughts and have some 'me' time. By looking up, you can change your perspective, and what's more you'll see what so many others choose not to see due to myriad different excuses and perceived time constraints that confront them. At any time you can get your Mojo working by stopping, relaxing, taking a deep breath and looking up when you are out. Whether you are running for exercise, walking for relaxation, whether you are at home or in the office, grab a cup of tea or coffee, sit back in your chair, and look up. Just try it!

i DON'T KNOW HOW SHE DOES iT

Michael Parkinson is one of my favourite interviewers. I believe he manages to draw more out of his guests than most television hosts. While interviewing pop icon Madonna, Parkinson recounted the story of one of her dancers going backstage after a performance and saying, 'I don't know how she does it, I'm stuffed, and I'm so much younger than she is.' Parkinson then asked Madonna, 'How long can you keep doing this?' Madonna quickly turned to him and said, 'I don't know, how long can you keep doing what you're doing?' Parkinson was momentarily stuck for words (which doesn't happen often), and Madonna went on to say, 'Why are you putting barriers on me? While I'm enjoying and able to do what I'm doing, why should I stop?'

This exchange really started me thinking about ceilings we create for ourselves with regards to age. Madonna calls it suffering from ageism. She believes that we get to a certain age and then we expect to change because we get old. In his book *Renewal: the Anti-Aging Revolution*, Timothy J. Smith MD says that the body is designed to live to be 120 years old. If this is the case, we definitely need to change our views on ageing in order to steal back our Mojo and keep it for the long haul.

I run marathons on a regular basis, and I am always staggered by the age of some of the people who finish ahead of me. For these people age is no barrier, and they certainly have a firm hold on their Mojo. Age is as much a mental barrier as it is a physical one. I'm not saying that certain things don't deteriorate as we get older, however I believe that deterioration is due mainly to the toxins and processed foods that we put into our system. If we stick to the guidelines discussed earlier in this chapter - drink lots of water, eat live foods, avoid processed foods, and exercise three to four times a week at the right heart rate zone - you can be full of life, totally coherent, energetic, and have the use of all your faculties at any age.

In order to steal back your Mojo you have to realise that age is just another obstacle that we have a choice to either accept or to reject. There are certain words that you may choose to erase from your vocabulary regarding age, and if you also take the right steps with food, nutrition, and exercise, you can live to a ripe old age, and love and enjoy the process!

DRiNK UP

One issue that people rarely consider when they lose their Mojo - their energy, spark, oomph and clarity of thought - is dehydration. Lack of fluids or dehydration can really impair performance, even when your body fluids fall just two per cent below the normal level. It's astonishing, it has been said that dehydration by just three per cent can drop performance levels by ten per cent.

The primary cause of dehydration in humans is sweat loss, an essential body process that facilitates the release of body heat. When you don't replace what is lost in sweat, the body's heat management system is compromised, placing both your performance and physical wellbeing at risk. Dehydration strains the cardiovascular system by reducing blood volume. This means the blood flow through our bodies and our brains can be hindered. This results in not only thirst, but also feelings of weakness, decreased performance, difficulty paying attention, headaches, fatigue, and feeling down.

Whether you are running after the kids, enjoying social activities, out and about with friends, in the workplace, training at the gym or running a marathon, dehydration can impact your Mojo in a big way, so keep it in mind and always have water close to hand.

Be wary also of mistaking dehydration for hunger (something I have been guilty of many times). When you become dehydrated you can often feel hungry, however in most cases you are not hungry at all, it's just that you are dehydrated and craving water. Unfortunately though, water mixed with scotch will not hydrate you, nor will a cup of coffee, or a can of soft drink. Alcohol and drinks such as coffee and non-herbal teas can in fact contribute to dehydration as they are diuretics and hence remove more fluid from the body. Dehydration also slows your reaction times and concentration, and decreases your decision-making ability.

One of the easiest ways to tell if you are dehydrated is the colour or volume of your urine. If it's clear or lightly coloured, you are fine, however if it is dark yellow in colour it is likely that you are dehydrated, although vitamin B tablets or multi-vitamins can taint the colour of urine. A reduced urinary output is also indicative of dehydration. If you're thirsty it is already too late, as thirst is your body's way of saying you are dehydrated.

The recommended amount of water that adults should drink each day is two litres. Now if drinking that quantity of water per day sounds a little daunting I would suggest that you always have a bottle of water on your desk at work, and put one or two glasses of water around the house so that every time you walk past you can take a sip. Don't think that by drinking a bottle of water in one go you have hydrated your system (if anything that can do more harm than good). You are much better off just having regular drinks of water throughout the day in order to keep your hydration levels topped up. If you can drink two litres a day, that's terrific.

Don't forget that if you are engaging in sporting activities you will need to consume at least two litres of water during the day, preferably more. Gatorade. com is a great resource for checking your hydration levels and has a university in America that monitors and researches dehydration. It's a good site to look at as a resource for understanding how dehydration can affect you and also how much water you should be drinking for your own particular body type.

So grab some water, drink up, and steal back your Mojo!

MOJO CHECK-UP

✓ Am I eating 70 per cent live food?
✓ Am I getting enough rest?
✓ Am I drinking lots of water?
✓ Am I exercising?
✓ Am I exercising in my target heart rate zone?
✓ Am I taking time out for me?
✓ Am I taking time to ponder and create?

CHAPTER 6
FOREVER YOUNG

I love the thought of being forever young. What a great premise! There's a gym that I head to each week and I have done so for the last seven or eight years. From my very first visit I remember seeing a silver-haired gentleman (who by now I would guess is about 65 to 68 years old) who is not only in terrific shape but also trains with guys half his age. This guy is one of the most sociable members of the gym yet he is probably the oldest male member by 20 or 25 years. During that time he has been working out with the same bunch of younger guys, and he pushes as much weight and has as much fun as any of the young guys in the gym. He prides himself on his condition and wears clothing that shows his physique to great advantage. Good on him! Here is a guy who is determined to fight the ageing process and stay forever young.

THE CENTURIONS

In *The Bulletin* magazine on 29 August 2006, the cover story was 'How you can live to be 100 and beyond - a special health report.' The article explained that scientists believe that the number of Australians who live to be 100 is expected to increase from 4000 people in 2006 to over 50,000 people in 2050. This group has been called the Centurions. New medicines are curing once-fatal diseases and medical breakthroughs point to a day not far away when instead of transplanting organs we'll simply grow them from our own stem cells. Last century 70 was considered old, but soon enough we'll regard 70 as merely middle aged. Our kids will break through the centurion barrier and live to be super centurions.

All over the country there are people in their 70s and 80s surfing, running marathons, driving across the country with their partners, taking holidays in exotic places and pushing the boundaries of age. This generation is determined to stay forever young and hold onto their Mojo until a ripe old age. Gone are the days of thinking that once you turn 50 or 60 you are getting old and your Mojo should drop away.

Now, of course not all 70- or 80-year-old people still have their Mojo. The difference between those who have and those who haven't is primarily a state of mind. It all starts and ends with the mindset we each create. If you have a mindset that you will be living to the age of 100, as I do, then you will take care of your body, your soul, your mind, your health and your spirit.

The brain is the only organ of the body that gets better the more you use it. The centurions who are still active in their 70s and 80s are walking, swimming and stretching every day in order to keep in good shape.

They're also doing plenty to exercise their minds through clubs, games, reading and an active involvement in the workforce. They not only stay physically fit, they keep fit mentally too.

Murray Rose, now 67 years old, was a triple gold medallist at the age of 17 in the 1956 Melbourne Olympics. He also won gold in Rome in 1960. He still swims three or four times a week at Sydney's Bondi beach, and competes regularly in swim classics. Murray Rose said, 'I don't think there's any secret, I swim in all conditions all year long.' People can fall into pockets of comfort, so you need to set yourself new goals and new challenges.

You are only as old as you feel, and you are only as old as you think you are, and if we are all going to live longer then we should start taking care of ourselves *now* to ensure we enjoy the journey. It's never too late to start exercising, and not only the waistline benefits. Dr Jack Cannon from Charles Sturt University has studied resistance training in the elderly and shown that even mild exercise using weights can increase bone density and muscle mass by 30 per cent. If it can work for the elderly then it can certainly work for younger people.

STATE OF MIND

Nothing will bring more Mojo to your life than aspiring to stay forever young. No matter how old you are now, it should be an attitude you adopt as one of your long-term goals. People ask me how I am enjoying having a new baby in my life, and I have to say it is one of the most wonderful gifts to have a baby in my 40s as I get to feel like a kid again every day. Blowing bubbles on my daughter's tummy is a wonderful gift, along with her continuous barrage of smiles, giggles, and gurgling.

Whether you stay young through children, through associations with community groups or charities, through family, hobbies, comedy clubs, the movies, or just dancing in a funny way when no-one is looking, don't lose the spirit of the child. Think young and you will stay young. Laughing, giggling, being silly and defying your calendar age are all great ways to steal back your Mojo. As I mentioned earlier in the book, I am a great believer of Madonna's philosophy on ageism. Just because the years may be passing doesn't mean that your Mojo needs to decline. Your calendar age and your Mojo age can be two totally different things.

STAYiNG CREATiVELY FiT

There was a study conducted in America some years back that measured the creativity and imagination of a two-year-old. The research showed that at the age of two children used 100 per cent of their imagination and creativity. By the age of five, the percentage of imagination and creativity the child was using dropped to 40 per cent. This is a staggering reduction, and one that would prompt you to wonder, what happened? I think most people would agree that it comes down to conditioning by parents, society and those around us. When children start hearing words like 'don't' and 'can't', they start seeing and hearing rules, and as a result boundaries and limits are put around their once limitless imagination. Now, here's where it becomes interesting. What percentage of imagination and creativity do you think the average 40-year-old is using? Just two per cent! It's not that the other 98 per cent has gone, it's just that we're not using it.

Staying forever young is one way for you to access the 98 per cent of creativity that is just not being used. It's still there, it's just that if you did some of the things you used to do as a small child, you would be seen as being immature and would probably be reminded to act your age. This is one area where those who are forever young would buck the system and refuse to act their age, as being forever young is all about doing the exact opposite. It's *not* acting your age, but instead finding a new way to defy age, have fun and find the spirit of Mojo, whether it be through hobbies, adventures, trips away, breaking routine, stepping out of the rut, or experiencing some of the things that you used to when you were a child - it's these things that are the spirit of forever young and that will steal back your Mojo.

In Chapter 1, 'Mojo Mindset', I discussed visualisation. It is possible to visualise yourself forever young in the same way that you can visualise yourself at any age with Mojo. Sometimes in a session I will have people write down what might be said about them during the speeches at their 80th birthday party. A lot of people can't picture themselves as being anything but old, a little senile, dribbling, and having a broken-down body. This does not have to be the case, unless it's what you want to see in your own mind. What is concerning to me is that most people are programming themselves for this sort of old age as opposed to an attitude of forever young where age is just a mindset. As the wonderful Joan Rivers said, 'You look in the mirror if you're over 50 and you have two choices, death or humour.' Now, there's a Mojo mindset!

Creative thinking, problem solving and finding a new idea or a different way of doing something can definitely spark your Mojo and keep you forever young. I love to see the glint in someone's eye when they've just had a great idea. Spark your imagination, unlock your great ideas, fire up your creativity and steal back your Mojo. Now in order to be healthy and promote wellbeing, we all know that we should exercise daily and we should eat the right foods and of course get adequate rest. These elements are critical to enhancing creativity. Apart from your body's general health and exercise you also need to start thinking about exercising your brain to promote Mojo and stay young.

You can exercise your mind with books, magazines or audio programs, brain teasers, crosswords, puzzles or the simplest of all, engaging in conversation where you ask a few questions and really think and listen for answers. Having your imagination sparked and your creativity boosted is a sure fire way of stealing back your Mojo. Yet in our time-poor, multitasking world, we don't spend enough time thinking, let alone exercising our creative minds.

In my first book, *The Keys to Creativity*, I discuss the creative process and the things we might do to stimulate our creative mind. From watching a quiz show, to playing a game of checkers or chess, or going to trivia nights at the local pub, there are plenty of ways that you can exercise, stimulate and stretch your creative mind. Albert Einstein said, 'The mind that opens to a new idea, never comes back to its original size.' And so that is also true for Mojo. Ideas, creativity and solving a tough problem are sure-fire ways of growing your Mojo.

Just like our sports heroes need practise in order to perform on game day, so does our mind. Whether you're a painter, a political leader, someone who works in community service, a golfer or a business leader, if you want to improve, you need to practise. I call it getting creatively fit. The more creatively fit we get our brains, the more likely we are to have our Mojo working and to stay forever young. The more you exercise your mind, the more you will enjoy the challenge of creative thinking and the better you'll become at it. Ask yourself each day, have I exercised . . . my brain?

CHAPTER 7

HOW DO i GiVE MY KiDS MOJO?

After speaking at a conference in London I was approached by a gentleman from the crowd who asked me whether it was possible for a dad to raise his children to have Mojo. I thought it was a terrific question. We had a brief discussion about the things that he could do to ensure that his child was given the best opportunity of having Mojo. I have spent some time thinking about this, and I have put together some advice to help parents raise their children with a sense of Mojo and to foster it as they grow up.

Firstly and perhaps most importantly, you need to lead by example. There is no question that children learn and absorb a lot of their personality and character traits from their parents. They are walking, breathing little sponges! If as a parent you are working 60 hours a week and then bringing home a heavy load or burden into the house, you can bet that in some way that is influencing your children. Those children who see their parents working so hard and being burdened with the worries of the world will naturally think that this is the way life is. If you're not taking time to think, ponder, enjoy, have fun, laugh and get your own Mojo going, you certainly won't be affording your children, who idolise you, the chance to be doing the same thing. Quite often when I'm speaking to audiences about creativity, one of the things that resonates most with them is how little time we as parents are dedicating to our children in order to foster their imaginations, creativity and problem-solving ability. Most parents are so busy that they don't take time to sit, laugh, play and engage in meaningful conversations with their children. Working up to 80 hours a week leaves little time for Mojo.

As mentioned earlier in the book, if you ask anybody anywhere in the world about the Crocodile Hunter, they will probably agree that he was the walking personification of Mojo. His adventurous nature, his attitude towards life, his *can do* attitude, his energy and the way he behaved and lead his family was simply outstanding. In the week following Steve Irwin's sudden death, his wife Terri was interviewed on Channel 9 by Ray Martin. During the interview Terri discussed how quite often Steve would get up in the very early hours of the morning, around 4 a.m., go to his office, work for a couple of hours, but make sure he was back in the house ready for the moment his children woke up. He would burst through the door, jump onto their beds and start playing with them. He'd then take them to the kitchen and feed them, while Terri was making the beds up in the children's room. Without even thinking, following breakfast Steve would take the kids into the bedroom, completely destroy the freshly made beds and make them into a cubby house! He just loved being a child and was not concerned about rules or what he should or shouldn't do. He was simply living in the moment, complete with Mojo. As I listened to the interview it made me think that he really is a shining example to all parents as to what's possible.

Steve knew exactly the sort of spirit he wanted his children to grow up with. You have to lead by example if you wish your children to follow you. If you yourself don't have a sense of Mojo in the food you eat, your mindset, taking time to think and ponder, or having a sense of adventure to try new things to get your Mojo going, then you certainly can't expect your children to do these things.

Unfortunately a large proportion of our children - it is said to be around 60 per cent - are overweight or obese. This is a direct reflection of their parents. A mother recently made a comment to me that I thought was particularly insightful. She said that a lot of parents are going shopping in supermarkets and buying junk food treats in order to keep their children happy. She believed these parents were substituting good old-fashioned love, attention, and affection with food in order to keep their children satisfied and engaged. They were using food to buy attention. If we are going to raise our children to have Mojo, then they need the same healthy food that we do.

GET THEM THINKING DIFFERENTLY

In the wonderful book *Einstein Never Used Flash Cards* by Kathy Hirsh-Pasek and Roberta Michnick

Golinkoff, these two psychologists give us valuable information about how to raise your children to have Mojo in the areas of creativity, imagination and problem solving. After extensive research in many different countries, their findings can be distilled into two critical factors.

The first one is *have a curious mind*. Ask your children questions and have them think about different options and solutions as to why things happen, what needs to be done, what they might want to do about it, and so on. A curious mind is a creative mind. Rather than just having conversations that exchange statements, try engaging in real and meaningful conversations with your children to get them used to asking and being asked lots of questions.

The second factor is *engage in play*. We're so busy in this world of multimedia we sometimes forget to stop and simply play with our children. Wrestling, laughing, chasing, running around, and participating in games are all wonderful ways to not only enhance the creativity and imagination of your children, but also get their Mojo working. And who knows, engaging with your children in fun activities may even help get your own Mojo going! The simplest solutions are often the best, and *Einstein Never Used Flash Cards* is a terrific read for anybody who is looking to raise their children with the spirit of curiosity and a powerful imagination. You will never look at toy shops the same way again!

When I was working with a law firm in Adelaide one of the senior lawyers told me a story regarding his stepson. He said each night his stepson asked him to read a story. One night, in the middle of a book, his stepson leaned across and closed the book, and said, 'What happened next dad?' As his dad went to open the book to continue reading, the stepson kept a solid grasp on the book, not allowing him to open it. He was forcing his dad to use his imagination to continue on with the story.

The lawyer said he'd learned a lesson that night, and now for ten minutes during each working day he closes the door to his office and writes down his own story. He said he loves this short break in the day where he can sit and really use his imagination to create a fictitious story for his stepson. Even as he related the story to me he had the biggest grin on his face, and he said he hadn't done that sort of thinking since he was in primary school. He said it with such excitement and vigour that there was no doubt he was enjoying the challenge of using his creative mind and imagination.

Giggling, laughing and playing are all wonderful ways to not only stimulate children's creativity, but also to get their Mojo going. The average child in America hears twenty times as many negative comments as positive affirmations. You can see why children are having the Mojo drained out of them from such a young age.

Many mornings I will be out with my young daughter walking, exploring, chatting and laughing. It's funny how many fathers I see going in the opposite direction pushing a pram. Invariably, rather than engaging in a meaningful conversation or enjoying a giggle with their child, or even sharing in the stimulation of the surrounding environment, the dad will be busy talking endlessly on his mobile phone. This is not only a missed opportunity to stimulate the Mojo of their child, but also a waste of valuable one-on-one time.

In his book *The Map of the Child*, by a pediatric cardiologist, Dr Darshak Sanghavi, he recalls that as a medical student on an oncology rotation years earlier, he noted that many patients with critical illness expressed regret that they hadn't spent more time with their families.

Don't be one of those parents. When you have the opportunity to engage in meaningful conversation with your children, give them the respect they deserve. If you take them for a play in the park or at a playground, then give them your full attention. Trying to eat a sandwich or talk on your mobile phone while keeping one eye on the child is not helping them to develop their Mojo.

Steven Spielberg once said that he had the majority of his ideas for his movies while at the dinner table with his seven children. Spielberg said that dinner-time was important family time where all nine of them - the parents and children - sat and talked. He also said he spent time asking questions of his children. Not only was it very rewarding for him in a family sense, but judging by the accomplishments of this movie director, you can see that the ideas that came from the dinner table were very successful and profitable!

SO, WHAT CAN WE DO?

Firstly, make the time to spend with your children. Yes I know it's easier said than done, but remember that we all have the same time available to us, it's about how you choose to use yours. Don't wait for a tragedy to happen before you say to yourself, 'I wish I'd spent more time with my children.' Approach each day like it's the last day you'll ever spend with them and you'll certainly reap the rewards. When people say they need to work long hours to support their family, they're giving away the best years of their life with their children. Are you really doing it for the family, or are you a workaholic?

In saying that, I think it's important to go back to the fundamentals. The Mojo mindset we talked about earlier in the book is just as appropriate for children as it is for mums and dads. We need to foster, grow and encourage a Mojo mindset in our children. They must be encouraged to look for options and they must know that it's not what happens, it's their attitude to what happens that makes the difference.

It is also critically important for us is to educate our children about food and how it can influence mood, energy levels and stress. I can't emphasise enough how important it is for us as parents to guide our children with the right nutritional information.

Our role as a parent is to encourage our children to be the very best they can be. In the book *Secrets of the Baby Whisperer*, Tracy Hogg makes a very important point when she states that your children are not yours, they don't belong to you. You've simply been given the opportunity to raise your children to be the best they can be. But our role as parents is to provide the environment as opposed to having them recreate in the same model as us. Each child is an individual person, and we need to ensure we create a great framework to help them to make their own decisions and ideally the right decisions, which will lead them to a life of creativity, imagination and Mojo.

I wonder how many mums or dads reading this book really see themselves as outstanding parents. Think about how you conduct yourself and what you're doing to inspire, educate and grow your children. Think about what you're doing to grow their Mojo. Think about what you're doing to inspire their imagination and help them to be the best they can be. Are you doing a good job, a great job, or do you hold yourself to the standard of an outstanding parent?

Everyone has it within them to be an outstanding parent; the first step is to consider and see yourself as being outstanding, and not just settling for being a good parent. Often it takes a tragedy or an unfortunate event for people to make changes in their life. If you're reading this book then you have the chance to make those changes now. If need be, re-read Chapter 2, 'Raise the Roof' and ponder it from the perspective of being an outstanding parent. It begins with you. The difference between a good parent and an outstanding parent is your thinking and your attitude. Naturally once our thinking is right, we need to do something with it, which is where willpower becomes a vital ingredient.

THE SCIENCE

There is a whole field of scientific study behind the concept of leading by example, particularly in the development of infants, toddlers and young adolescents. In their first year of life, if a child is stressed the most likely cause is that the parents are stressed.

In the research that was done for the ABC television show *Life At 1*, parents were asked how often their household is stressed and in most cases the response was 'always' or 'often'. Every household is rushed or time pressured at some point, but when it becomes a constant stress it can damage a child's brain.

When a child is stressed the body produces adrenalin. If the child remains stressed, then the body starts to produce a chemical called cortisol. Cortisol is released by excessive stress. Cortisol shuts down the areas of the brain that control memory, thinking and immunity. This constant stress and constant level of cortisol slows the development and growth of the brain. When a child is one year old, it will have developed 50 trillion connections in the brain. By the time the child is three years old, these connections have increased to almost 1,000 trillion. However, it is around this time that the brain begins to lose the connections that it is not using. When a child is constantly stressed, the brain shuts down those parts of the brain that it does not see as essential to cope with this high stress level, and the areas that are shut down are those areas largely responsible for the development of creativity, imagination, problem-solving ability and ideas. As these parts of the brain are shut down, the lower part of the brain develops strong emotional connections, and in some cases, the child is more likely to become aggressive, lacking in remorse and unable to understand the consequences of their actions.

Healthy brain development is not about flash cards and Mozart, it's about providing a consistently warm and loving environment. Do this and you will set your child on the path to happiness. When bringing Mojo into the life of your child, the fundamentals are as simple as the act of cuddling, cradling your child and most importantly establishing eye contact with them. A child that is loved and nurtured develops strong attachment connections and is more likely to be a healthy, happy, outgoing, contributing member of both your family and society with their Mojo working.

There are two other quite startling footnotes that are worth mentioning to any parent who's reading this chapter. In the documentary *Life At 1*, it was noted that those skilled professionals who worked long hours scored themselves poorly when asked to rate themselves as a parent. There are two issues going on here - firstly, the standards you hold yourself to as a mum or a dad, and secondly, your priorities. The second note from the documentary is that they believe there is also a link between childhood obesity and the amount of exercise that the child's parents do. So before you put down this book, just have a think about how much exercise you've done in the last fortnight and whether or not you are in fact leading by example. Because if your Mojo is not working, you can be sure your child's won't be either.

MOJO CHECK-UP

✓ Am I leading by example?
✓ Am I setting the example I want my kids to follow?
✓ Is the household stressed?
✓ Do we talk, laugh and create together?
✓ Am I stimulating my children's imagination and curiosity?

CHAPTER 8

KEEPiNG iT GOiNG

One of the points that I always like to address towards the end of a presentation or speech is *keeping it going*. People always enjoy reading a book or going to a workshop but find it challenging when two weeks later they have a quiet moment of reflection and seemingly find themselves back in a rut. It's at that point that you look in the mirror and think 'Who stole my Mojo?' This chapter will summarise the tips that keep the momentum going and keep your Mojo strong.

COMMiT

None of the tools, tips and techniques in this book will amount to anything unless you commit to using them. If you've reached this point in the book and you are thinking, 'I'll *try* to do this' then I'm sorry to say you are defeated before you start. As Yoda, the Jedi Knight from *Star Wars*, says, 'Try, there is no try, there is do or do not.' The first step you must take in order to find, keep and foster your Mojo is to make a commitment to do so. Mojo is a way of life. It shouldn't be something you either have or don't have. It is something that is within all of us, but like anything it needs to be worked at constantly. Of course there are going to be days where you just won't have your Mojo going, but the important thing is to make a commitment to yourself that, should that be the case, you'll take some time out, rest, slow down and regroup. It's hard to have your Mojo going 24/7, however Mojo is a mindset. Commit to having a Mojo mindset and you'll find it much easier to regain your Mojo if for some reason it starts to slip.

Remember everyone is creative. Everybody is talented. But not everybody has Mojo. But then you're not like everyone else - and that's *your* choice.

SET YOUR OWN STANDARDS AND REMOVE THE CEILINGS

To get your Mojo working you must do something today that is different from what you did yesterday. A lot of this comes down to the standards you set for yourself and how much you like to challenge yourself. If you settle for mediocrity and a world of bland then that's exactly what you can expect to get. Consequently it will be hard for you to be excited about your world, and your Mojo will be less likely to be stimulated as a result.

In order to have your Mojo working you need to set standards for yourself that constantly challenge you and push you forward. If you are not challenging yourself and stepping forward then you may find yourself stuck in a rut and hemmed in by routine. Don't settle for mediocrity and a world of bland - challenge yourself with small or large goals that will excite you, break your routine, and push you forward. One of the ways to do this is to constantly ask yourself questions. Use your primary questions, challenge yourself mentally and stimulate your curious mind.

Another way to keep your Mojo going is to make sure you do not allow fat bastards to enter into your thoughts. There's no doubt that those voices will appear from time to time, but you can control them before they steal your Mojo. Remember that it's not what happens that is important, it's your perception and opinion of what happens that shapes your mindset, and your Mojo mindset is completely within your control.

MAKE MOJO TIME

If I can encourage you to do one thing, it would be to open up your diary each day and allocate Mojo time. Allocate time to stimulate your creative mind with a walk, reading time, a puzzle, exercise or a conversation with a good friend in a coffee shop. You can stimulate your Mojo each day by incorporating some creative thinking and imagination time. We've talked about slowing down and the Mojo mindset. As Da Vinci said, 'A busy mind has no room for creativity.' My belief is that if time is not set aside in your diary each day, chances are it simply won't happen. Prioritise your thinking and regrouping time.

Whether it's five minutes, ten minutes or an hour, make an appointment with yourself for Mojo time.

SHAKE iT UP

There is no doubt that Mojo is stimulated when the mind is stimulated. If you find yourself back in a mundane and bland routine then that will suck your Mojo. Each week or each month, make sure you do something that is out of your comfort zone in order to shake up your routine. It could be as simple as going to work a different way or visiting a different restaurant for lunch, reading a magazine, going away for a weekend, or doing something extreme that challenges the adventurous side of your personality. Do something each week or each month that makes you a little uncomfortable. Perhaps make a list of the things you've always wanted to do in or around your own suburb, city or country, and systematically work your way through that list during the year ahead. Shake up your routine. Do things differently and you'll set yourself on the road to Mojo.

JOURNALiNG

As a final action plan for you, if you haven't already done so I would strongly encourage you to buy yourself a nice journal. There are some beautiful journals available in bookshops and stationery stores, and I'm sure you'll find one that is appealing to you. Whether it's places visited, people you have met, comments about experiences or just mental notes about random thoughts or occurrences, journaling is a wonderful way to capture and stimulate your imagination and your Mojo.

One other powerful use for your journal is in those moments of self-doubt or at a down time when the fat bastards find their way into your mind - it's nice to be able to pull out your journal and read about the people, places and events that have been positive and fulfilling, to help quieten the voices of the fat bastards. Sometimes we're so busy focusing on getting through the day and worrying about the future that we forget to reflect on the positive and happier times from our past. While we shouldn't dwell on the past, we should take note of some of the great things and use them to fuel the present moment and take us towards the future. I find it helpful to have a journal on my bedside table so that each night I can just jot down a few notes. I have several journals I use for different reasons and I keep them scattered all over the place, from my bedside table to my office to my travel bag. I always make the time to record random notes, ideas, concepts and comments from people, movies or books that I would like to keep for reflection.

TEXTURE

A friend of mine says that throughout life you're going to be hit with good and bad, happy and sad, delight and disappointment, pain and closure. Yet all these experiences add up to form the texture of your life. This made me think about some of the great photography I've seen over the years, like portraits of old people where you can see the stories and texture in their eyes and expression. It's a wonderful thought that the story of one's life is made up of texture. The highs and lows, the good and the bad all make up the story that is our life. And without these peaks and troughs one's life could really be rather bland and mediocre. Every great success story has its triumphs and disasters that make up the texture or the story of your life. The important thing to know is that when you're feeling down, disappointed, or your Mojo is simply not working, there is a way to steal it back.

GET BACK TO THE BASICS

Working in the corporate world I am constantly amazed at how many organisations book speeches and creative sessions to develop the next great idea for customer service. Yet right in front of them are the fundamentals which in most cases are not being met. If we could just get the fundamentals right in the first instance we would have immeasurable impact on our personal lives, business and Mojo. It would take us a long way to raising the roof and providing outstanding results.

As an example, not long ago I was enjoying a cup of coffee over a one-on-one session. The owner of the cafe that I was visiting went to great lengths to explain to me how fantastic his coffee was. He spent five minutes explaining the special blends, how he put it together, the history of it, how he presented it and altogether trying to create a great experience in my mind for the espresso I was about to enjoy. After sitting for about an hour enjoying our coffee, the owner of the cafe started walking around the table impatiently. I noticed him walking around, and I said to him, 'Would you like us to go?' He very abruptly and sternly snapped at me, 'Well I've got people waiting,' and stormed off.

Now I can fully understand his desire to get as many people through the cafe as possible, however the unnecessary snap and attitude that he displayed towards us had me leaving with a bad taste in my mouth. The sad thing is he put so much effort into his coffee and was so proud of his brew, yet he forgot one of the fundamentals of customer service, and that is to make the customer feel great, to smile and to provide an attitude that would invite me back to his coffee shop.

The reason for this part of the book prior to finishing is to remind you to always get the fundamentals right. I hope that you found this book full of interesting and useful tips and tools for stealing back Mojo. But if I could make one recommendation before you put this book aside, it's to always remember the fundamentals and go back to basics before anything else.

So what are those fundamentals? The first one is checking in with your Mojo mindset. The reason I enjoy working with people is that all action, results, execution, strategy and personal achievement starts from thinking. Problem solving, creativity, imagination, it all starts in the mind. As the famous cartoon character Pogo once said, 'We have met the enemy and the enemy is us.' When you feel that you're starting to lose your Mojo, check in on the fundamentals and ask yourself the question 'What am I focused on, am I focused on the right things?'

The next fundamental is your nutrition and exercise. Quite often we fall off the wagon and find ourselves on a downward spiral of the wrong foods combined with little or no exercise. So if you feel your Mojo slipping away, check in on your mindset and make sure you're feeling groovy. If you're not, clean up your diet and start exercising. These two things alone can make an immeasurable difference.

Another fundamental to consider is the people around you. Sometimes people get so caught up in their work that they forget about those who are most important to them. This once again can put us in a downward spiral and often it can take a sad event or a shock to trigger us to remember how important our friends, family and council are to us. Having said that, beware of the fat bastards in your head and the fat bastards around you who try to pull you down. It's not what they do or what they say, remember, it's your mindset and your thinking that makes it so.

The last fundamental to remember is to hold yourself to a standard higher than anybody else could possibly hold you to. When you find yourself falling into a rut, the world of bland, or an unexciting place that's not stimulating, then raise the roof, set new standards and take action. Most people create ceilings for themselves that hold them back from being the best they can be. You probably don't know what you're capable of. Don't die wondering. Have a crack, remove the ceilings and raise the roof.

SO HOW DO YOU KNOW YOU'VE GOT iT?

There's probably no real way to know when your Mojo is working at its best. I think it's just a feeling. We all know that feeling when you return to work after a holiday, and you have a clear head, lots of energy, you look great, feel great, and you're firing on all cylinders - well, that's Mojo. It's that day when you wake up in the morning with confidence, vitality, zest, a spring in your step and a glint in your eye, and you hit the office on fire. Nothing that anybody says or does that day can take that feeling away. That's Mojo. It is also that moment in the middle of a game of soccer or a round of tennis, when no matter what you do you hit the ball sweetly and no-one can stand in your way of victory. That's Mojo. It's that afternoon when you are lying on the floor, playing with your baby and your heart is exploding with the unconditional love you share. All seems right with the world. That's Mojo.

To me, Mojo is a feeling that you know when you have it, and you certainly know when it's not happening. Hopefully the tips in this book will help you to get to that place. We all have a different definition and a different feeling of how we measure when our Mojo is working, but my belief is that everyone has been there at some point in their life, and by following the tips that I've given to you in this book, and using them as stepping stones, you will get back to that place again. I believe it's very hard to have your Mojo working 24/7 all year round. It's something that does at times get stolen from you, or that you can allow to disappear. And maybe at times, that's okay. There are also times when you just want to *be* and don't need to have your Mojo working. The important thing is knowing that when the time is right you have what it takes to access your Mojo and get back in the game. It's all to do with thinking, and for me it's an inside job - inside your head. Don't let fat bastards or anyone else steal your Mojo. Don't lose it through poor nutrition or lack of exercise and don't program yourself to look at things the wrong way.

Herb Elliott, one of Australia's greatest ever athletes said, 'Enthusiasm gets you started, but habit keeps it going.' I hope that these tips and tools will allow you to constantly refresh your memory and try new things. My suggestion is that you take a tip or a couple of tips each week, try them, put them into practice, and the next week try something else. Don't try to do it all at once. Take small steps each day to get your Mojo working. And if in two weeks, a month or six months time you're sitting on a bus or staring at your computer wondering 'Who stole my Mojo?' just remember - you did, and at any given time you can steal it back! So what are you waiting for? Get your Mojo working and get back into the game of life!

LAST THOUGHT . . .

When your Mojo is firing and you are around people that do not have their Mojo going, be aware that it is possible to come across too full on, and in some cases, scare our friends or acquaintances and not intentionally, turn them off. You need to be careful that although you are on the path or have already reached that state, that you don't inadvertently force your opinions or energy on those that aren't ready for it. Obviously the reason you chose to pick up this book or read it because someone recommended it to you, was because you were ready. Not everybody is ready at the same time. Stealing back your Mojo quite often only happens when an event provides the spark. You're fortunate that for whatever reason you now have the knowledge and tools in front of you to enhance your Mojo or in fact, steal it back. Although you know that everyone has the Mojo within them, some people are just not ready for the message. Keep this in the back of your mind when sharing or helping others. Our tone, manner and general excitement can sometimes be a huge force and a great help to others, but in the same way, it can also be a case of bad timing.

Who Stole My Mojo? is about you, your thinking, and your Mojo. Simply by being your best, removing the ceilings, eating well, having your thoughts in the right place, and going about your business, you will unquestionably influence friends and those around you without knowing it. As Oprah Winfrey said during the introduction to the ESPN sports awards, when she presented the award for courage, 'The single greatest thing any of us can do is to empower others.'

RECOMMENDED 'MOJO' READING

The Keys to Creativity, Gary Bertwistle
The Juice Master, Jason Vale
The Power of Full Engagement, Dr Jim Loehr
The 10 Rules of Sam Walton, Michael Bergdahl
Nothing is Impossible: The John Saunders Story, Gabriel A Kune
Secrets of the Millionaire Mind, T Harv Eker
Anyone Can Do It, Sahar Hashemi
Slow Burn: Burn Fat Faster by Exercising Slower, Stu Mittleman & Katherine Callan
Slowing Down to the Speed of Life, Richard Carlson & Joseph Bailey
Renewal: the Anti Aging Revolution, Dr Timothy J Smith
What It Takes to be #1, Vince Lombardi Jnr
NOW: No Opportunity Wasted, Phil Keoghan
Why We Want You to be Rich, Donald Trump & Robert Kiyosaki
Rich Dad Poor Dad, Robert Kiyosaki
The Barefoot Investor, Scott Pape
Einstein Never Used Flash Cards, Kathy Hirsh-Pasek & Michnick Golinkoff
Secrets of the Baby Whisperer, Tracy Hogg

APPENDIX

Allocate your action or thing you will implement into six stages, so that you are not endeavouring to do everything at once. Space out your plan into weekly/monthly increments in order to maximise your learnings and actions.

Stage One Plan:	Stage Four Plan:
Stage Two Plan:	Stage Five Plan:
Stage Three Plan:	Stage Six Plan:

My Council

Work/Business	Play

Words to Erase

Work/Business	Play

NOTES

ACTIONS

WHAT	BY WHEN

NOTES

ACTIONS

WHAT	BY WHEN

NOTES

ACTIONS

WHAT	BY WHEN

Also available from Capstone

ISBN 9781841124704

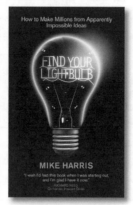

How to Make Millions from Apparently Impossible Ideas

MIKE HARRIS

"I wish I'd had this book when I was starting out, and I'm glad I have it now."
RICHARD REED

ISBN 9781906465049

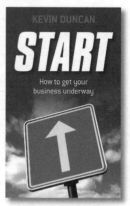

KEVIN DUNCAN

START

How to get your business underway

ISBN 9781841127941

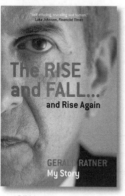

The RISE and FALL...
and Rise Again

GERALD RATNER
My Story

ISBN 9780470694442

The ACCIDENTAL PORNOGRAPHER
Gavin Griffiths

A story about having a go and succeeding... in failing.

ISBN 9781906465254

Read this book if you plan to be an entrepreneur, find out what it's really like before you make the leap!
Doug Richard, Entrepreneur and business investor

?

SO YOU WANT TO BE AN ENTREPRENEUR?

HOW TO DECIDE IF STARTING A BUSINESS IS REALLY FOR YOU

JON GILLESPIE-BROWN

ISBN 9781841128030

CAPSTONE
be inspired!

An Imprint of WILEY
Now you know.

For more information regarding Gary Bertwistle,
The Vault, or any of Gary's keynote sessions,
please visit www.garybertwistle.com.

To have Gary speak at your next conference or team
session, please contact the office on 02 9356 4280,
or email info@garybertwistle.com

BERTWIST E

Also available from Capstone

ISBN 9781906465018

ISBN 9781841127330

ISBN 9781841127118

ISBN 9781841127439

ISBN 9781906465445

ISBN 9781906465322

ACKNOWLEDGEMENTS

Thanks is too small an acknowledgement to the three most important women in my life - my beautiful wife Emanda, my angel daughter Charley and of course my mum! I can never thank you enough, I love you guys. My greatest appreciation to the backbone of my business, Gabbi and Shay. You guys are the Mojo behind the company and not a day goes by where I don't appreciate you and everything you do for me and the business.

To the guys who kick start my Mojo each day at 4.30 a.m., the Tour de Cure peleton. Cougar, Devo, Disco, Kosi, Pantani, Learjet, DL, Max, Hipster, Freddie and the rest of the crew, what can I say but 'Regulators Mount Up!' To my agent Carolyn Crowther, no-one would ever get to read this book had it not been for you. I'll never forget our first espresso coffee together and it certainly won't be our last. My sincere thanks to all the guys at Allen and Unwin, Ian Bowring, Andrew Hawkins and Fiona Wilson, for the belief, guidance, energy and espressos! I am proud to be a part of your team and appreciate you taking a chance. And to anyone who has ever sat in the audience of one of my keynote presentations and given me a smile, a nod of the head, challenged me on something, given a thought-provoking question, a round of applause or a compliment, my thanks for giving me the greatest gift, by allowing me to do what I love to do and be rewarded in so many ways for it.

iNDEX